Social Media Marketing Live

Discover How Live Video Streaming on YouTube, Instagram and Twitch Can Help Supercharge Your Business Growth in 2020

By Rory Ames-Hyatt

Table of Contents

within this document, including, but not limited to, — errors, omissions, or inaccuracies.

Introduction

Chapter 1: Social Media Marketing Explained (And Why Should You Care About This Digital Marketing Revolution?)

Chapter 2: Why Is Social Media Marketing So Powerful at Grabbing Our Attention?

Introduction

Have you had a good look at social media lately? Not a single Facebook video can be watched without at least one ad. Sometimes, there are even more. There are few to no YouTubers without sponsors, and Instagram has become a book of advertisements. The fact is, none of these platforms can survive without sponsors or ads. Streaming, on whatever platform, is a guaranteed view if done in the right way. The suggestions pop up, the ads redirect. The truth is, without social media, a lot of companies would topple to the ground.

Social media live streaming has taken brand marketing to the next level. Platforms, such as Facebook, Twitch, YouTube, and Instagram, are rushing to include live streaming to their sites. Brands, on the other hand, are slowly dropping the traditional ways of pre-recording their content for future use.

Social media marketers have not been left behind. Social media marketing has seen significant changes that will take this platform to the next level. Due to its proven track record, more people are likely to embrace this marketing strategy. Research done by Brainshark, a research company that deals with matters of social media, indicates that 93 percent of all marketers across the world have used social media to promote their brand. Another interesting statistic indicates that 74 percent of all internet traffic is in the form of video content.

Social media is an affordable, yet powerful, tool for marketing. If you are looking to take your business to the next level, social media is one factor you should not overlook. In context with live streaming, companies can utilize social media as a customer care tool or marketing tool. In this book, however, I am going to be focusing on how your business or brand can effectively market your services or products using live videos.

Let's face it. People prefer viewing video content over written content. This is because of its affordability and accessibility. One of the easiest ways to increase awareness for your brand is by engaging your audience through live streaming. In some media channels, your viewers can engage with your live videos and offer real-time, instant feedback. Take a moment to open your Facebook account and look at the composition of your newsfeed. You will find that out of ten posts, six or more are in the form of video.

So what does live streaming offer marketers? It removes the imagination customers often have about some brands.

And how has live streaming changed the way stories are conveyed? It offers a human-to-human discussion about a product. By asking questions in real time, your viewers will connect with your brand more.

At the end of your live stream session, what are you looking to achieve? Here are some things you will need to consider before choosing the most suitable live stream platform for your brand:

- Do you have the right filming tips, hosting styles, and various video ideas for this platform?

- Do you know what kind of target audience you are trying to reach?

- Do you know how much it is going to cost to run a live stream video?

- Do you know which platforms offer live streaming content? For example, in this book, we will be focusing on the following four live streaming website platforms:

About Facebook

Facebook is a popular live streaming platform. Even though this platform provides both written and video content, its popularity makes it a good choice for video-focused social media marketers. The number of Facebook users across the world had reached over two billion at the end of 2018.

About Instagram

Instagram is another popular social media platform which specializes in sending video and photograph content. This platform is most suitable for businesses such as fashion and food. It is not restricted to these two industries; it can work for various other industries. All you need is creativity. It is pretty simple to use this platform. As soon as you create your account, you are free to begin uploading videos. Your followers will start seeing your updates where they will then be able to like or make comments.

About YouTube

YouTube live is another popular live streaming platform. Even though this platform has been around for quite some time, its popularity has grown immensely since 2016. Research done by Market and Markets predicts that YouTube will be worth around $70 billion by the end of 2021. YouTube expanded its reach to select mobile phone users, explaining the increase in YouTube viewers since 2016.

There is no better time than now for marketers to promote their products on YouTube Live. In this book, I am going to take you through the various ways and the best practices for using YouTube. To fully capitalize on the returns of this platform, it is essential to learn the simple tricks and tips to making YouTube Live *really* work for your brand.

About Twitch

Twitch is another live stream platform that offers marketers an excellent opportunity to promote their products. This platform has two million users. Even though this number seems relatively small compared to other live streaming platforms, viewers spend up to one billion hours a month on Twitch. Another important statistic on this platform is that 90 percent of all views on this platform are attributed to only the top 5,000 streamers.

Twitch is a massive live streaming platform marketers should take seriously. It is slowly gaining popularity as an effective place for brand new influencers. And unlike other social media platforms, Twitch offers marketers a session of up to five hours of viewing. Another significant benefit of using Twitch Live is its interactive nature. It provides real-time interaction via live chat when the live stream is running.

Chapter 1: Social Media Marketing Explained (And Why Should You Care About This Digital Marketing Revolution?)

What Is Social Media Marketing, Really?

To begin with, social media is an umbrella term for all platforms that offer radically different social actions. For example, a social media platform like Twitter allows you to share short updates with the world. Facebook is a larger social network that incorporates the sharing of updates, videos, and photos, as well as many other things.

Now, social media marketing, often abbreviated as SMM, is a type of online marketing involving the creation and sharing of content through social media platforms and websites. The goal of social media marketing is to create content that will be shared by social media users with other people in their network. Unlike any other marketing tool, social media marketing has transformed the marketing world.

While digital and electronic marketing is still dominant among scholars and players in the marketing field, social media marketing is becoming even more popular with both researchers and practitioners. Social media has been touted as the greatest marketing tool ever created! And if that's hard to believe, here are some facts to back up that big claim. While the internet gathered its first one billion users ten years after its creation, Facebook crossed two billion users a decade into its existence—that means Facebook grew at double the rate of the internet itself! So, it's no secret social media is beginning to take over the world and revolutionize modern culture. In the United States, for example, 62 percent of the whole population use the Facebook platform.

Statistics in other countries are equally as staggering, and the growth is on a steep rise. Perhaps what has helped social media marketers most of all on these different platforms, however, is the presence of built-in tools for analyzing data which enable brands to keep track of the progress, engagement, and success rates of their marketing efforts. Today, businesses use social media to address areas such as their current and future clients, existing and future employees, bloggers, journalists, and so on. On a strategic level, social media marketing entails managing a campaign, creating a scope, governance, and establishing a company's desired 'tone' and 'culture.'

Social media marketing also provides start-up and struggling companies with the ability to market cheaply, a useful part of any marketing campaign. Unlike other forms of so-called 'traditional' marketing, such as radio, television, print, and mail, social media marketing's greatest advantage is found in a specific advertising metric known as Cost per Thousand Impressions (CTI).

CTI is essentially a way to measure how much money it costs for your ads to be viewed by 1,000 people. Compare this to traditional marketing methods. Although many people receive and read print versions of ads, like say in a newspaper, these readers don't necessarily view the newspaper ads before throwing them away. Social media ads, however, work with posts from other sites to increase the chances of your ad being seen - really seen - by your target audience. Social media, therefore, offers one of the most effective methods of ad placement out there.

Mobile phones have become quite instrumental in social media marketing. Today, over three million people are active across different social media platforms each and every day. As mentioned before, 62 percent of US citizens have active Facebook accounts. Eighty-one percent of the US population has some form of social platform they use regularly. Mobile phones and social media marketing are somewhat intertwined since most current mobile phones have social networking capabilities that allow people to interact with the world.

With the rapid growth in mobile phone usage, your average consumer's path-to-purchase has been fundamentally changed since customers can now access a product's pricing and other related information instantly. Social media has also become a powerful resource in acquiring marketing information as well as users' perspectives. Through content communities, forums, and blogs, individuals can share their reviews and recommendations about products, services, and brands.

A business that doesn't understand the worth of social media regarding brand promotion and customer interaction is hard to find. Social media marketing has become the core of countless brands' digital strategies and is handy in delivering clearly defined results in customer service, leads, and sales. And all the while, social media platforms are continually evolving as new features are released to boost engagement and customer experience.

A Quick Social Media Marketing History Lesson

Before the recent growth in social media platforms monthly visitors, marketing via social platforms was presumed to be a passing fad. However, when Facebook started gaining ground in 2004, internet users increasingly began to pay attention to - and copiously use - social media websites, and companies began to sit up and take notice. Nowadays, social media enables both small and large businesses to gain attention without having to spend a ton on marketing.

Before the advent of social media, the pioneer internet denizens in the 1980s used social networking sites (online forums and dating sites) like Livejournal, Six Degrees, and Friendster. These were the earliest forms of social media platforms. Between 1995 and 2002, the dot-com bubble played a critical role in allowing the internet to become a profitable marketing tool. First, brands began establishing their online presence in what has come to be referred to as 'search marketing.' As companies like Google, MSN, and Yahoo improved their search engines, brands turned to Search Engine Optimization (SEO) to enhance their ranking in the search engines. According to Search Engine Land, a definitive website for search engine basics, SEO is "the process of getting traffic from the 'free,' 'organic,' 'editorial' and 'natural' search results on search engines" (2019). Also, blogs, or web 2.0, became more popular during this period, prompting marketers to tap into the potential of online content marketing.

The years 2003 and 2004 were some of the greatest years for social media marketing. During this period, Facebook, My Space, and LinkedIn arrived and initiated a shift of online users from gaming to networking sites. Soon, brands recognized the positive results of social media marketing and began creating branded profiles on the most popular platforms. As time passed, the favorable attitude of customers towards online marketing began to change the preference of business marketing from an aggressively proactive approach to reactive inbound marketing.

In 2006, Facebook opened up its platform to the wider world and brands rushed in to create their profiles, ushering in the new era of social media marketing. Both consumers and marketers added to the market to increase the overall value of the social media platform.

The growth of social media is primarily linked to the growth in communications technology that accrued towards the end of the 20th century. In terms of time, the history of social media is arguably short. However, this doesn't make it less influential or exciting. Social media has grown steadily to become an integral part of people's lives worldwide.

Before the growth of social media, marketing used to require time-consuming and hands-on labor. Today, marketers are highly skilled. The changes notwithstanding, today's marketing requires far more complex strategies than even the most established marketers can execute on their own.

Why Is Live Streaming About to Take Over the Social Media World?

Live video is real and easy to connect with. Unlike written content and recorded videos, live videos add a human touch to advertising. The *New York Times* surveyed the type of content viewers prefer, and the result was astonishingly in favor of live stream content. Eighty percent of viewers prefer live stream content as opposed to written blogs.

These platforms compete for customers. For marketers, the best option is to explore all platforms when promoting the company's brand. Another difficult task for companies is maintaining a consistent social media presence. There is a perception out there that streaming your content across all social media platforms is a difficult task. It is simple. But first, before I go into more detail about how you can begin using live streaming content to grow your business or brand, I am going to explain some of the best practices for growing your organization's presence on social media.

A Quick Guide to Social Media Marketing - Best Practices and Tips

Currently, there are some exciting changes happening in the world of social media. And even in 2019, many social media platforms are still adapting to learn more about their user base, constantly tweaking their programs, algorithms, and codes to compensate for the huge consumer demand for their services.

Therefore, you need to create an online digital marketing strategy to help you cope with the ever-changing and developing world of social media marketing.

So here are some tips and ideas to help you launch and/or grow your social media profiles:

Make Sure You Have a Plan

Having a clear plan of execution regarding how to approach the craziness of competition on different social media platforms should be one of your top priorities. Using social media marketing is more of a marathon than a sprint.

So, slow down before leaping into the fray and make sure you have clearly identified your goals. For example, are you aiming to increase brand awareness of your business? Or are you simply looking for a way to scale up revenues? Keeping your end goal in mind is key when planning out your social media strategy.

Also, when planning for your first live stream broadcast, you should try to stick to a script and keep to a regular schedule. Such an important moment should not be the time for you to wing it. When you have a plan, you won't have momentary lapses of silence when shooting your live stream videos.

Advertise Your Brand

Before you can get all excited about selling and making money, get your brand out there to the people. Make the people know about your business or brand through advertising. Make the customers need your services or products. When marketing your business, you should realize that promotional messages are not effective on their own. So, you need to put yourself out there with your products. When selling your brand, you should put some soul into the process to help humanize your efforts.

This will make your business more relatable to the customers. In addition, social media, just as the name suggests, deals more with personalities rather than the products. People should find you more relatable than the product itself you are trying to sell. Also, remember, as the marketer, you are the face people will relate to in regards to the product you are selling.

Different trends are always popping up on social media that your customers will find relatable. This means you will need to look out for the hashtags and phrases that are trending. These will make your brand relevant to the younger generation on social media who are the primary target for most products.

Build Your Followers and Customer Base

One of the most important facts about social media marketing is that your ideal customer can always be found online. Without that fact in action, the whole idea of social media marketing would flop. So, you need to think about growing your own loyal social media customer base. Start thinking about how to plan on growing your follower count and keeping them engaged. Engaged followers are going to be the ones who will help share your brand with other people on these social media platforms.

Promote Your Social Profiles Offline

Adding the link to your social media accounts for products or flyers will help spread the word about your business. They will also pique the interest of potential customers who are not already following you on social media.

Understand Push Notifications

Push notifications, for those unfamiliar, are essentially pop-up messages that look to mobile users like SMS notifications. Now whenever you launch a live streaming session, your followers will receive a push notification message alerting them on the event. Keep in mind, it is important to consider if your audience will have the free time at that moment to even watch your event.

Note, catching your audience unaware may work for you or against you. Some viewers through curiosity will watch your video, while others will be too busy. Still, as a general rule of thumb, try to avoid business hours or late evenings when people might be sleeping. The best time to run a live streaming event all depends on the time zone in which the main bulk of your followers are live. In other words, don't live stream in London time if your main clientele are based in New York. Be smart and think ahead.

Utilize the Power of FOMO

The Oxford dictionary defines FOMO as the "fear of missing out." However, social media removes the fear of missing out on an exciting event by allowing users to always stay plugged in and aware of 'breaking news' and events. This is why social media live streaming is such an exciting development; you can live stream around the globe in seconds, capturing the real-time attention of as many viewers as possible.

Make Engaging Content

People want to see exciting things they don't see every day so try to make your content and videos as interesting as possible. It is worth noting that going live on social media is all about creating a real-time dialogue with your audience, so try to keep them engaged by having quick Q&A sessions or just by talking to them about trending issues in your industry.

Each social media live streaming platform has its own unique way of giving its audience a way to express their feelings about a session. Facebook allows viewers to give their comments below the video. Instagram, on the other hand, allows the audience to click a heart sign that represents likes, and even YouTube has the like, comments, and dislike options. Your viewers have to be drawn in by your on-camera personality and the quality content you deliver. Make the viewers enjoy giving feedback and do what you can to answer most, if not all, of their questions.

If you have to include content that is seemingly dull to many viewer - like excessive product information - consider adding additional elements to your work, such as giveaways and other rewards for faithful and new consumers.

Try Out All the Platforms (Don't Become Attached to Just One)

At the end of the day, every social media platform has its strengths and weaknesses. Ultimately, it is up to you to understand which one best suits your brand or business. People often rush to the most popular platforms only to realize later that a less popular platform would have worked much better for them. It is easy to say this, I understand, but research is key. Doing enough research on every platform - listing the pros and cons and deciding which platform will be best for you - will make a significant difference.

For instance, looking for an audience based solely on past consumer interest may be a mistake. Instead, consider new avenues that will excite new audiences. Consider joining forces with another large-name company or paying affiliate marketers for the benefit of wider audiences. Many people on Instagram, YouTube, and Facebook with large numbers of followers will feature your work or services in livestream videos for a fee.

A Quick Guide to Live Streaming for Absolute Beginners - Best Practices and Tips

In this section, we will be looking at the various ways live stream marketing can become a major contributory factor to the growth of your business, especially as live streaming is one of the best ways to build strong customer relations with your audience. So first, I am going to give you a quick rundown of the best practices for running your own live stream session, no matter the platform:

Practice Ahead of Time With Test-Run Videos

When you get on camera for the first time without making any preparations, you will be disorganized. Therefore, you need to make proper preparations by filming a trial video.

Prepare Your Pitch

Most people might think live streaming is a great way to simply jump into pitching themselves to customers right away. However, you should avoid doing this at all costs. Instead, you need to first make sure your viewers are comfortable and then slowly draw them into your show by warming them up and engaging with them at a personal human level. Your pitch - whether it be a product, service, or simply asking them to follow your brand - should only be mentioned casually from time to time throughout the stream.

You should also be ready through preparation to politely answer any of the customers' questions. If you cannot answer immediately, prepare an answer where you instead ask the customer to make further inquiries and call your business phone number, direct message you, or send you an email.

Use the Right Social Media Medium for the Right Message

You need to have a clear idea ahead of time of who your target audience is if you want your live stream to find your ideal target customer/follower. This information is of extreme importance when trying to decide which platforms to run your live stream sessions on.

For example, is your ideal customer under 35 years old and based in the USA? Well, then Instagram Live is one of the best places to reach them.

On the other hand, is your ideal audience member someone over the age of 50 and based in the UK? In that case, you probably have a better chance of reaching them via Facebook Live.

You then need to take into account which format your ideal audience prefers. Are they visual learners, or do they prefer more traditional text-based learning? Instagram has a user-base that engages more with visual concepts than text. On the other hand, Twitter has many more text-users than video, picture, and visual concepts. However, Facebook balances all the visual and text concepts into one well-trafficked platform (which is handy since Facebook has more active users at any given time than most of the other social media platforms).

Multiple Live Events Is the Key to Live Streaming Success

Try to choose the most optimal time for your live stream. It is a difficult decision to make, especially if you are looking to market an international brand. Time zones vary from country to country. And even though some of your customers are ready to burn the midnight oil, most viewers will not wake up in the middle of the night to watch your video.

The solution to this problem is doing multiple live events to cater to most of your viewers. Some companies, however, are limited to only one live event because of time. In this scenario, the perfect time to go live is the time zone most of your audience is in. Make an announcement on what time you will be live; this will help your loyal audience plan to join you for your live sessions, regardless of their differing time zones.

Keep Your Batteries Fully Charged!

Before going live, ensure your device's battery is fully charged. It seems like such an obvious thing to check pre liveshow, but you would be surprised by the number of social media live stream presenters who forget to do this pre-show check!

So, if you are using a desktop, you should have a fully-charged laptop on standby so you can quickly switch devices in case of a blackout. Also, note that a live stream taking 15 to 20 minutes is likely to consume as much as 20 percent of your laptop's battery life.

Experiment With Different Ways of Engaging With Your Audience

A good way to work out what works (and what doesn't) when it comes to live streaming is to research how other people have run their own successful live streaming projects. This way, you will always have a steady supply of ideas and show concepts for you to try with your own audience.

So, be ready to experiment with your ideas if you feel they might be a hit with your customer base. This means that the notion of live streaming as a marketing strategy has a lot of leeway you can exploit. You should not be shy of going after what you want.

Use live streaming to get to know your customer better. Incorporate more human interactions with your customer, gain their confidence, and, most of all, build trust.

Plan, Plan, Plan!

Always have a clear plan for your live streaming shows to work off of, but be sure it allows you some flexibility, too. In other words, you should remember that your show's plan should not be a strict final copy you show to the world, yet it is always worth being prepared. It's an old saying, but it bears repeating: "Fail to plan and you plan to fail."

Try to Get Feedback from Your Live Streaming Audience

One of the most important things to remember once you decide to take on live streaming is that constructive criticism from your audience is the key to helping you create better live streaming shows in the future. Therefore, you shouldn't get upset about receiving criticism that is less than favourable about your sessions. Take them on the chin, learn from them, and use them to make your shows better going forward.

Place Your Audience's Opinion Front and Center

An important part of any business marketing strategy is to show your customers you care about what they think. So, coaxing out the openings of your live streaming audience should be something you do throughout the stream. Moreover, you should also mention that you appreciate the fact that they've taken the time to watch your live show. You should tell them that you value their feedback and are working on implementing their advice towards improving your future live streams.

To do this, though, it is necessary to make feedback a two-way communication. In other words, don't simply tell your audience to give you feedback and then not answer their comments or concerns. A 'personal' bond with your live stream viewers will go a long way towards connecting with them and building brand loyalty. At the end of the day, no one is going to turn up to watch your live streams if you remain distant throughout the stream.

So, throughout your live stream you should be free and approachable. Make sure you sneak some funny content into your material, as well. Strive to make your audience comfortable. Also, most people do not like the notion of explicit material. Therefore, you should avoid this depending on the audience and the product or service you are selling. You should also remember to include and respect the different beliefs of people and their principles. Note that this is a good reason why you should carry out research on who your target audience is ahead of time.

If this all sounds a little daunting, it needn't be. It isn't hard to show your viewers you are just human and not some corporate hotshot. Everyday folk dislike corporate stiff because they do not feel comfortable with them - it's all just too formal and feels inauthentic. So, try to add in some casual fun shows, say, record a game night with your co-workers as a live stream show. This way you can show your audience that your company is all hard-work, but that you know how to have fun, too.

Different Live Streaming Content Ideas You Can Use for Your Business

As I stated earlier in this book, an important part of any social media marketing strategy involves planning, and live streaming is no different in this regard.

So in this section, we are going to cover a few live stream content ideas that you - as a business or solo entrepreneur - can consider when planning your own show's content:

Live Stream Industry Interviews

Most companies nowadays prefer the idea of conducting live stream interviews. You can, for example, run live streaming interviews with your employees who can in turn give your audience better insights into the inner details of how your company or business works.

These types of live streaming interviews show your customers the kind of culture your business has. However, make sure the employees you interview live are decent, stable, and approachable. The image of your brand is very important, and so you should protect it.

Customer Care Services

One of the major logistical conundrums of any company is customer care service. You need to have people on call who can handle the needs of your customers at all times of the day. However, the manual way of conducting this service (for example, having a dedicated member of staff available to answer phone calls or emails) tends to take a lot of time that could be used elsewhere in your business. Taking care of customer service through live streaming saves a lot of time that could be used for other clients' needs.

You could run a weekly live stream show where you can help multiple customers - most of whom may be dealing with the same problem - all at the same time. You could also employ the method of hosting a training seminar on how to use your products. Or, you could train the customers in where and how to behave when they visit your company for help or business. This helps to avoid confusion within the business. Also, you could offer a training course for the employees who are lacking the skills for selling your products. They don't have to visit the headquarters of your company. Therefore, using social media live streaming in this way can make for an incredibly cost-effective teaching tool you can use in your business.

Gather Customer Reviews

In a good business, especially in the food industry, it is good to have a critique of the service and the food you offer. Consequently, you should use reviews to help you grow your business's brand. So, once in a while, why not host a mini-preview party for your customers via live stream? Your customers will happily tell you about everything bothering them, as well as give you ideas for how you can offer them a better service.

However, not all of your customers' recommendations will prove applicable to your business. Therefore, you should look out for the ideas or problems pointed out to you that are directly critical to the progress of your company and handle them immediately.

Also, during these preview parties, take the time to ask your customers what will make them happy. How would they like to be treated in the process of dispensing care and products? This Q&A party will help get you to the truth of all the adjustments you need to attend to.

Be wary of customers who enjoy stirring the pot, though. We all know these exist. They are the ones who like causing trouble, giving bad reviews just to get free stuff (with no intention of giving your product or service an honest review). So be sure you know the difference between constructive criticism and pot stirrers, and handle each accordingly. Taking constructive criticism will be great for your business, but handling bad reviews in bad taste will leave an even larger impression, and not a good one. When you are live streaming and doing a Q&A, be prepared for anything and have a smart and witty, but not too, arrogant comeback for everything. No one likes a jerk, but shutting the troublemakers down with confidence and manner will make your loyal customers buy a lifetime subscription to your brand.

Offer a Sneak 'Behind the Scenes' Peek at Your Business's Operations

This is one of the topics we looked at in the previous chapter. It is paramount that you show your customers how you operate from time to time. This, in turn, builds trust with the clients. Also, you should live stream about how the products are made and how the services are being offered. This will give the customer a sense of belonging. They should feel as if they are part and parcel of the company's operations. Use this opportunity to set the expectations of your customers. For example, you could walk around your shop and show the availability and low prices you have in your store. Again, you can show the customers you are willing to negotiate the prices of the products.

"Nothing is too much for you," is basically what you are saying, and that is what a customer wants to know. Knowing that a business will go the extra mile is what will make them pay the extra dollar for whatever you are offering.

Introduce New Products and Services

Introducing new products and services is one of the best ways to exploit this modern-day live streaming marketing strategy - and it is a way for you to get your product out there faster and cheaper than ever before. You can also use this opportunity to teach customers about the product and its benefits. You can take the chance to showcase any improvements you have made to your service. Don't forget to urge them to try any new products or services that you have introduced to the market.

For example, at one time, GE (General Electric) made the point to introduce one of its electric cars through live streaming on Facebook. Immediately, the car took the social media community by storm. Almost everyone was talking about it, and many people wanted to get their hands on one of the cars. Many people also left comments, and it had over 56 thousand views during the live stream. It was later shared on the internet, and millions of other people watched to see what all the fuss was about.

Even the people who do not use social media heard about the news because they focused on the right platforms and viewers. Launching a new product or service via live streaming can really push your product or service further than ever before, but only if it is done correctly.

Live Streaming Stumbling Blocks: Examples of When Live Streaming Goes Wrong

Live streaming will not always be a smooth process. It is essential to understand that some things could go wrong in the process of recording. It is important to understand some of these errors. Here, I illustrate each one, as well as how you can mitigate these errors right away.

Technical Errors

While it is important to put most of your emphasis on the content of live streaming, beware of some of the technical errors that could occur during the actual event. These technical errors could occur from either your end, or your viewer's end. To ensure you don't experience a sudden break in internet connection, choose the time of your event wisely. The most common cause of network breakage is extreme weather conditions.

Inconsistencies

Don't you just hate it when a streamer is inconsistent with his content on some videos? This is the result of poor planning, and it could lead to some very embarrassing situations. Planning is key, and this I cannot stress enough. Be sure you know what you want to say and when you want to say it. Be sure of your facts and don't jump around.

Terrible Questions

Remember what I said about handling those live Q&A pot stirrers? This is exactly where that comes in. If you are live streaming and doing something where the viewers are interacting with you, this is one of the most common things that could go wrong. Have those answers ready.

Stage-Fright

This is a real thing even when you are on camera. Freezing during a shoot is not rare, but the way you recover is key. Stuttering is the first sign that you are experiencing stage fright. Take a deep breath and collect your thoughts. It's scary to think that you will be live to thousands of people. Stay cool and don't let the fear ruin the whole experience. If you are uncomfortable, your audience will be, too.

Lack of Promotion

We know what you're thinking. The point of live streaming should involve audiences. But what about those who are busy at work, are out socializing, or are even simply sleeping?

Picking the right time of day is one of the most important parts of marketing. Promoting an event that takes place at 3 A.M. for a target audience will keep you from getting those few remaining views. So, set the time up well in advance for your live video. Spend time analyzing when to best meet your audience. Live questions can be just as important to the video stream as the content you present.

When done correctly, live streaming can be fun when marketing your brand and engaging your audience. If the above errors are taken care of, your live stream event will be a success. These errors can be quickly be fixed and knowing exactly what could go wrong is a huge help to avoid them. Avoiding is better than fixing, but if the error occurs, fixing it quickly is best.

Social Media Strategizing: Key Things to Consider When Creating Your Own Social Media Marketing Strategy

Having a social media platform should never be a choice for any marketer; it should be automatic after establishing your business. Having a clear strategy is also essential; it is key if you want to achieve your marketing targets. Consequently, you need to have a plan for which channel or platform you want to use. After that, you need to know what type of content to post.

Another important thing you need to consider is the type of audience you are targeting with your products. You need all of this information, before you start creating your marketing strategy, in order to have a proper response plan to the numerous questions your audience will be asking you. Also, you will need a plan for how frequently you will be answering the customers' questions.

Reliability

If you plan to be a social media manager, you need to have some steadiness with your work. Plus, consistency is essential because it will help you keep the customer's attention. Therefore, you need to put regular posts on your channel. Also, you should keep the content of your social media posts as fresh and entertaining as possible. Having fresh and fun content on a regular basis will ensure that viewers will be coming back for more, and that is what you want. You want your loyal viewers to stay loyal and bring new viewers with them. They won't recommend an unreliable source to a friend. This goes for the people in your employment, as well. They have to know you are reliable, and in that way, they will talk to their friends which will give you positive exposure, too.

Developing and Sharing Your Content

Creating and developing social media content is one of the major steps in managing a social media account. You will have to write and come up with fresh ideas to appeal to most social media users.

However, from time to time you can share content from another account. When sharing other people's content, you *always* have to give credit to the original owner. Also, you can use phrases like "#stolen" if you don't know who the original owner is. To include the owner of the content, use the share button.

This is great for getting involved with the community and showing that human side we've spoken about earlier. You want the people to know you are 'among' them and the act of sharing their posts is perfect for that.

People are keen to have a look at whoever shares or likes their posts which, surprise-surprise, gives you exposure. If they follow the link to your account, chances are they will want to have a look at your profile and what you have to say.

Keeping in Constant Touch With Followers

Keeping in touch with your followers means you have to answer the numerous queries they may have. Moreover, you should have the habit of routinely checking the comments section of your account to see what your followers have been up to. You don't have to respond to everything, but the more you do, the better. You should look at the matters that are most pressing and respond to them first. You should also try to respond to questions within 24 hours (or even less!) and always endeavour to give your best and most authentic answers to hard questions and comments.

Reach Out to Other People In Your Industry

By now, you should realize that managing social media goes beyond just responding to followers on your page. You must find time to engage and interact with other people on their pages, as well. Also, you will need to look for ways to network with other people in your niche or industry. Basically, you should aim to try to build a business relationship with others who are doing the same social media brand building work as you. By doing so, you will get an opportunity to share ideas and marketing strategies with them that can mutually benefit you both.

You also need to consider reaching out to offer help, strategies, ideas or advice to social media influencers in your niche. They, in turn, can help increase your popularity in social media circles by encouraging their followers to follow your account. This will help your business's name spread even further and help grow your customer base.

Basically, your aim in networking online via social media outreach is to try to make friends in strategic places. You have to systematically put yourself out there (and into the direct messages) of potential friends who can help you take your brand to a whole new level. You do this by first finding mutual ground and helping them out where you can, because when the time comes, you have a favor to reel in. Note, don't use them, but make it clear that it is a 'you scratch my back, I scratch yours,' type of deal.

Hosting Campaigns

Hosting social media campaigns is one of the essential ways to help market your brand. Also, it will help you in answering the various questions your customers have been asking. Through these campaigns, you will target a specific type of follower so you can deal with their problems or simple issues. The campaigns will help you reach new people who are not yet following you online.

Hosting Contests

Hosting contests is a great way to keep your customer base interested in your website, brand, and/or products. Consequently, you will need a clear cut plan to host your contest and giveaways. You will need to be clear about the rules and regulations of your giveaways (and stick to them come what may) to make sure the rewards and giveaways are given to the people who deserve them.

Contests are also great for attracting new customers. Once word spreads about basically *anything* up for grabs, people will compete from all over the world if you intend on making it international. In turn, it will give your company the exposure it so desperately needs.

Keeping Records of Performance

Always keep records of your social media activities and expenditure. By doing so, you will make sure you do not waste time on tactics that are not bringing in good results for your business. It will help you to realize if your efforts are working or not. You can act early to alter strategies in case what you are doing isn't working for you. You shouldn't be afraid to try new things.

If the new ideas fail and the records show that the old ones were doing better, don't be afraid to revert. New is always good, but don't throw away something solid for something new. Keep an eye on the performance records and decide which of these makes your clients happier. If neither work, perhaps taking an entirely new route is the answer. Be smart about it.

Social Media Management Explained

Social media management is basically the organization and management of all your business's or brand's internet activities, content, and interactions through social media platforms.

Some of the more popular social media platforms include YouTube, Instagram, Pinterest, Twitter, and Facebook. However, you should note that social media management involves more than simply posting a quick update on your profile or your company's profile. You should also try to interact with your followers and friends. This way, you can make sure you have a good working relationship with your customer base. Therefore, if you need help to market your products and services, they will come through for you at all times. In the process, you need to be looking for new ways to increase your brand's visibility and reach.

So, in order to get the most out of your social media management skills, you have to consider which is the best social media platform to use. For example, you should know that if your target audience is comprised of people who like visual content, then you should use Instagram. Also, you should remember that Instagram has more young female users than male. So, it would be a good platform to promote, say, the fashion industry.

On the other hand, Facebook has a larger number of people at any given time. Also, the users are from different backgrounds, and the gender balance applies to its platform. It is the best platform to reach a larger customer base.

YouTube, on the other hand, is another larger social media search engine, second in size after Google. It can help you by giving a platform where you upload your videos as a marketing strategy. What's more, is that it can host video ads to help sell your products better.

Chapter 2: Why Is Social Media Marketing So Powerful at Grabbing Our Attention?

Nowadays, technology has become an essential part of everyday life. Most people, regardless of age, gender, religion, or race, highly rely on it. Also, you should notice that technology has engulfed the communication world and is one of the fastest developing fields in modern life. This means that technology is making the lives of humans easier, which is obvious by the electronic gadgets used in support of technology. Likewise, the use of social media continues to increase in growth and development.

As the demand grows, social media platforms have to come up with ever more efficient ways of serving their users, and so the platforms of social media are constantly adapting and changing for their target audiences.

For example, social media is one of the current tools most people and companies use for marketing. So, this brings us down to the use of technology in the form of social media. When and why can we explore the use of social media, especially in the area of live streaming, to help us in marketing?

The concept of live streaming involves airing one's views or ideas through media platforms like social media to people around the world. You can also say that it is the process of transmitting live videos through the internet for anyone who is online to see or listen to you in real-time.

So far, as of 2019, only a few of the major platforms offer live streaming, such as YouTube, Facebook, Instagram, and Twitch, among others. But live streaming is one of the developments of the 21st century that help small businesses compete with major ones on a global scale, allowing you free access to a marketing tool that is more akin to to getting TV advertising time at peak hours - but without the high costs associated with that more traditional marketing outlet.

Why You Need to Start Live Streaming: Understanding the Marketing Power Behind Live Streaming

In this section, we will be looking at 8 key reasons why you should use live streaming for your business or brand:

1. The Concept of Transparency

Most people always want something in which they can trust. So, most of the time, when you are buying a product, you should look into the trustworthiness of it. Consequently, you should be completely transparent when dealing with your customers. You will drive your customers away if you do not open up about the services and products you are marketing. For example, you can use the live streaming process to air how your products are produced and marketed. However, you need to get the consent of the customers before live streaming their opinions on social media. By doing so, it opens your business up to constructive criticism that will, in the end, help you improve your business. Through live streaming your services on social media, you will attract more customers.

If you are selling a certain product, why not open it on camera and show the viewer exactly what they will be receiving upon purchasing this item. This way, the packaging along with its contents can be discussed and handled by you in front of your current and potential customers. This ties into transparency, as the item is exactly as advertised with no filters, no professional photographers, and no ad companies. People want the real deal.

2. Cost-Effective Marketing Platform

One of the biggest benefits of live streaming as a marketing strategy is that it saves money. Sometime back in the day, most businesses had to buy air-time on television and radios to market their platforms. However, since the invention of social media and live streaming, advertising has become more economical.

You will have to make a one-time investment on the equipment to broadcast the platforms to the world. You can also look for professionals who can help you run your live streaming sessions. The services of these professionals are not as expensive as in TV and radio advertising.

This being said, you don't want it to look like a 1970s auto sales commercial. Professional doesn't mean fake. It merely means the content and quality have to be solid.

3. Managing Product Criticism

The world of social media is an open platform for critics. If you get negative reviews on social media live streaming, take it as a chance to improve your business. Most of the feedback you get from social media is instant, therefore, as a good business person, you have the time and opportunity to make improvements and accommodate your customers' needs.

Be careful not to change your image too much to accommodate the critics. Your original customers have been loyal to the product you have been delivering and to the marketing strategies you have already mastered. Don't lose your original clients because of a small critique that will do nothing to improve your service or product.

4. Cashing In on the Attention of an Ever-Growing Audience

At any given time, there are over one billion social media users actively using one of the top four social media platforms: Facebook, Instagram, Youtube, and Twitter.

And what this means for you, as an entrepreneur, is that these marketing platforms always have eyes and ears waiting and willing to be engaged with new information and ideas at all times of the day.

Therefore, the world has migrated almost fully into the digital marketing world of social media. People in the live streaming world have the ability to share the content of your live streaming with other users. They can invite others to watch as you live stream, or they can simply hit the share button. This draws attention to the ever-growing and active market of social media.

Since your content can be seen anywhere in the world, this broadens your marketing base from local to international markets at just the click of a button.

5. Providing a Source of Entertainment

Live streaming is one of the concepts most social media users find quite thrilling. They feel as if they are a part of the process that is taking place no matter how far away they are. So, when you make your content and share it with the public, you should try to find a way to inject a little humor. The viewers of your content will make their thoughts known directly in the comments section. You could hold polls or contests to entertain and engage the people who are watching your live stream. All in all, the process of live streaming should be a thrilling and entertaining marketing concept, enough to keep your viewers interested. Having fun is more often than not the key to successful streaming. If you, as the streamer, are having fun, your audience will automatically adapt to your mood. Laughter and jokes are the best type of entertainment, but don't overdo it, either. Say what you want to say about your products or services, but don't be stiff. Joke around every now and then or make a video solely about having fun.

6. Customer Care

Live streaming is one of the ways that has helped to deal with the issue of a service providing to your customer base. It reduces the time and work of the service provider. This is because as a service provider, you bring together customers with similar problems and address them at the same time. In addition to that, it helps you save your customers' resources and time, too. It is a tedious feat. I will not lie and say that it is not. You will have to deal with a lot of rude customers and the odd online troll. Don't let them get the best of you, as the way you handle them will have an effect on the other customers, too. There's a lot riding on your customer care tactics.

7. Introducing New Products or Services

In today's world, the concept of live streaming new plans for your business should be like a sixth instinct. As has been discussed above, you can reach more people through social media live streaming. So, you should make the most of your announcements about your new products or services through live streaming. Moreover, it will make the customer feel as if they are involved in the progress of the company. This usually builds trust between you and the customer.

You can give all your loyal customers exclusive access to the live streaming before the general public can access the same. They will appreciate it. Plus, you can go one step further and offer your live streaming audience reasonable discounts off your products or services, particularly when you're introducing a brand new product into the market. The use of live streaming services allows you to show your customers the various ways to handle your products.

You can also use this time to show your customers the various ways you offer services at your company. This will boost your customer base by enticing and appealing to the needs of your customers at all times.

8. Showing Customers How Your Products Are Made

Today, people have so many varied notions about what they want in their lives. For example, some believe they should not use certain materials or chemicals, and so they tend to be more cautious about what to eat, what to wear, or even what to use. So, if you are promoting an item produced with the use of natural elements, you could use your next live streaming session to show your customers exactly that. By doing so, your customers will begin to believe in the products they are buying, as well as the ethos of your brand or business. All of this helps you build a trust-based relationship with your customers and/or social media audience.

You could also show them the shopping process of the items they order and how they are handled from stages of packaging, shipment, and when they receive it. All in all, you should keep in mind not to live stream elements of your company that are likely to put you in a hard position. Therefore, it will be essential to seek legal advice about how to proceed with live streaming, especially if you are working with a big company that has to stick to very strict industry-related by-laws.

The Process of Live Streaming, Simplified

As we have seen above, live streaming can be an especially powerful part of any social media marketing strategy. But that still begs the question: How, exactly, does one go about setting up a live stream? What equipment do you need in order to run a live stream smoothly? Is there a general process to follow or can you jump straight in? These are some questions newbies need to ask themselves before jumping into live streaming as a marketing tactic.

Plus, it is always worth remembering that in order to achieve marketing success, you need a solid plan based on clear fundamentals. Moreover, you should be flexible with your plan and allow it to compensate for any hiccups that may arise.

One of the most important tips when going through with your plan is to keep everything natural. You should remember that the concept of live streaming humanizes you. The customers will feel as if they already know what and who they are dealing with. The idea of live streaming can only work if you have a large social media base to rely on. This is never the case for most people when they are starting out.

If you don't already have a decent sized social media following, you will need the help of social media influencers. These are people on social media who have many friends and followers. They can help you host a watch party for their fans, followers, and friends. Thereby, they will endorse your product or services to their social media base. You should also remember to do your research to target industry-related influencers who are willing to help your specific business niche. However, if your business is already booming, you could instead hire a professional to handle all of this for you. It will be their responsibility to manage networking with influencers, plan the live stream, and organize everything else so that you can get the very most out of every live streaming session.

Remember that consumers can market for you. That's the beauty of social media. Unlike other forms of marketing, consumers who tag you or your product in their posts will be doing the marketing for you. They will invite others to look at your product or service information, making your consumers your most practical and useful asset. Therefore, frequently giving your customers "shout-outs" to show your appreciation for their loyalty will go a long way for creating a positive image of your company. Including these shout-outs in live streaming videos is an excellent way to show you're connected with your customers.

You should remember why you are live streaming. Therefore, you have to remember to mention your product and its benefits to the customer. Above all, you should make sure your customer gets to know how the service or the product operates. If they watch the live stream and, at the end, fail to comprehend the need for the product or service, then you have failed as a marketer. As I have mentioned before, you should also try to sell a feeling to the customer.

The emotional concept of live streaming will capture the attention and the hearts of many people. However, you should try to research your audience to find what makes them tick. This is to avoid making the wrong pitch to the wrong crowd. Offer your loyal customers incentives. This may include a discount or a gift for valued, frequent buyers of the product or service.

So, all in all, when you are making the live stream video, it should serve the needs of your customers. In business, a satisfied customer is a customer for life.

Live Streaming and Social Media Advertising: Can You Run Paid Advertising on Your Live Streams?

Yes, you can use ads on your live stream. One of the major concepts of live stream marketing is the use of ads. When doing the ads, you should make sure the video you are making is of good quality in every way possible. You should remember that having a bad video in your live stream can be harmful to your brand, so you have to be good at it. If you cannot do it yourself, then consult a professional to lend a helping hand. Also, you should make adequate preparation and practice to help you get the proper tone to your video. Some also say it is important to have aesthetic value in your videos. This will capture the attention of the customer. They will watch your video and decide if the product is good or not.

If you manage to capture people's attention on the internet and sell your products, they will share with their friends who will also share with others. Therefore, your product or service will have a larger market base to help you make bigger and better sales.

Estimating the Price of Live Streaming: The Three Main Factors That Will Decide the Cost of Running Live Streams

If you consider marketing your products or services through live streaming, you have to bear in mind the cost of the entire process. There are various factors to take into consideration when calculating the price of live streaming. For a person who has just begun, assessing such factors could pose a challenge. The factors include duration, complexity, and equipment, as well as live streaming services.

Complexity of the Live Stream

The more complex the live stream is, the more expensive it will be. A complex live stream would probably use numerous audio and video sources. There might also be numerous locations of the same event and the signals from the various locations must be delivered to a central location, which might require a production team or, at times, an engineer.

Simple live streaming, on the other hand, is quite affordable. Just imagine a stream involving only one camera; for instance, a smartphone camera in conjunction with simple overlays and graphics. You can broadcast such a stream regardless of how tight your budget is.

Still, take the time to consider how many sales you will be making with a complex stream compared to a tight-budget stream. If the number is significantly higher and the profit is worth it, don't waste your time on a low budget production.

Duration of the Live Stream

A stream that takes a long time is more expensive. Costs such as bandwidth, a venue, as well as staffing, add up with time. A stream that runs 24 hours a day in the form of a TV channel needs production-grade appliances, staffing, and a metric-ton load of bandwidth. In such a situation, consider streaming the videos on platforms that have a powerful live streaming CDN.

A longer running stream also runs the risk of becoming tedious and boring, so perhaps cutting a 20-minute video in half and uploading more frequently will be your best bet. Personally, I enjoy a short, powerful video more than a long, stretched out one. I find myself losing interest and becoming distracted with things other than the stream.

Cost of Live Streaming Equipment

As anticipated, the more streaming equipment required, the higher the cost of the live streaming. High-quality equipment will also make your business incur higher costs. Today, broadcast-quality equipment is affordable. Nevertheless, it is crucial that you ensure you consider your equipment needs when budgeting.

Rather, aim a bit higher and know that you won't have teenage garageband quality sound and video. Quality is always your best bet.

You can also incur further costs based upon which live streaming platform you decide to use. Fortunately, you can elect to use a professional-grade platform for streaming that is powerful, as well as affordable. There are similarities and differences between the various video live streaming services, being either professional or consumer-grade video platforms. Sure, you could use a free platform, but it may be worth taking a broader look at whether they will either help or hinder your business.

For example, free live streaming services may be unsuitable for professional users for numerous reasons. First, free platforms come with advertisements. They heavily monetize the content found in videos to suit their benefit and not yours. For instance, your content could be placed to appear next to the advertisements of your competitors. Your content could also be mixed-up with advertising not even related to your broadcasts.

Secondly, free platforms are also commonly known for blocking content. For example, YouTube is among the websites that involve heavy blocking worldwide. Most schools, businesses, universities, and many other entities entirely block access to such sites.

Thirdly, the free platforms do not offer professional-grade tools for your streams and videos. Monetization, customized branding, and security settings are all either absent or rudimentary. Therefore, you should rely on platforms that have professional-grade streaming.

Live Streaming Equipment: What You Will Need

Camera Equipment

One camera alone can have a great impact on the cost of live streaming by reducing expenses. Nowadays, smartphone video cameras are cheap and reliable, but be prepared to pony up the cash to pay for a decent smartphone with a quality camera. Nonetheless, many businesses and some pro-level streamers opt for dedicated cameras. If you are planning to stream your video only once, and you still need a video that is pro-quality, you will have to hire a company for video production. Such a company may provide the requisite audio equipment and camera, thus saving you from investing in equipment that is costly and unnecessary for long-term use. The cost of live streaming cameras ranges from free, through a smartphone, to $4,500+ for a TV broadcast-quality camera. You can also buy a camera that is solid and mid-range and has a good quality video for about $2,500.

Audio Equipment

A video camera with an in-built mic may be sufficient for simple live streams. For professional use, you will need better audio equipment. This may comprise of lapel microphones, Omni-directional microphones, or directional mics. Also, you will need cabling. If you have various audio sources, mixing will require specific equipment. The cost of audio equipment range from free, to $4,500+ for a complex setup. You can also purchase a small setup that has microphones of high quality for less than $500.

Encoder

The cost of software meant for live stream encoding can range from free, to approximately $1,500. Additionally, a software encoder requires a computer for proper operation. If you are streaming a complex video that requires a multi-camera stream, along with animations, you will need a powerful computer with quality hardware. Some software encoders are free and can run on computers starting from around $500. On the other hand, software encoders of high quality cost about $3,000.

Technicians and Staff

Other than equipment, you will have to consider the price of live streaming staff and technicians. Bear in mind, each camera requires someone to operate it unless you want PTZ cameras. You will also need an individual to mix your stream. Hiring them will be expensive. It's therefore advisable to use an in-house IT person or technician to be economical. The cost of staff varies, depending on the experience and location.

Importance of Live Stream Marketing for Your Brand

Nowadays, most businesses opt for live streaming due to the benefits it offers to not only the businesses, but also to the consumers. First, live streaming helps in the growth of your audience. This is because there are billions of people on the internet. Live streaming grants access to consumers who failed to participate in the forums, announcements, question-answer sessions, or any other event your business has hosted.

Live streaming also has the positive effect of reducing costs. Some companies rely on live streaming for training programs to train overseas employees. Every person gets the same product information and training at the same time, hence saving the company money. Also, when hosting a live event, the cost of travel, security, and lodging is high. Choosing a live stream for the purpose of airing a certain event, instead of the live event, will save you a lot of money. The money and time you save will permit you to spend a lot of resources and time on the promotion of your products and the growth of your brand.

Live streaming also fosters audience interaction. Having face-time with the consumers will allow your brand to link with its audience and allow you to effectively tell the story of your brand. If your business engages in live streaming events alongside question-answer sessions, this will permit the participation of viewers at home. Using live streaming for marketing your brand will aid you in developing a trusting relationship with your audience. Live videos come with certain vulnerabilities. Those who are not rehearsed appear more realistic, trustworthy, and relatable. This is an expression that your business values transparency and is not scared to reveal its true identity to consumers.

Through live streaming, your brand will have the chance to inter-promote and interconnect its platforms. For example, you could encourage your live stream audience to tweet any questions they may have and also 'like' your Facebook page. This will effectively grow your presence in social media with those who are interested in your brand.

Furthermore, live streaming serves as a suitable platform for reinforcing your brand's values. You should deal with a live stream just like you would with another medium of marketing because you are airing your voice to the entire world. What is the message you want to deliver to the world about your brand? What ought to be the 'takeaway' for your viewers? Utilize your live stream video to make an attractive impression and show personality to your viewers, however, ensure you do not entirely convert it into a pitch for big sales.

Laying Down the Law: Legality Considerations of Live Streaming

The amount of video content put out on social media platforms has increased over time. And as the number of people watching videos has grown, so has the amount of red tape and legality surrounding posting any video on a public platform.

However, what's allowed can vary depending on the social media platform you are using. Live stream videos related to television programs and sporting events are illegal. Numerous laws deal with copyright, and taking a wrong step will result in heavy fines. The location of your live streaming is the most crucial thing, and it is, therefore, good to be aware of whether you have the right to carry out live streaming in your place of choice.

For example, it may be okay to film on public property, but there may still be exceptions. And even though a street can be deemed public property, you cannot barricade traffic to record your video.

There are also restrictions about taking videos within the environments of a court or a school. Even though most schools are situated on public land, laws have been set to protect school-going children from predators. Commercial live streaming by influencers on social media and within businesses have the prerequisite of obtaining a permit.

Other (non-legality related) laws governing social media apply to live streaming, as well. Consider the following:

1. The Law of Influence

This involves making an attempt to find online influencers in your market who have audiences that are of quality and a high possibility of being interested in whatever services or products you are marketing. You ought to connect with such people and work towards establishing relationships with them. In the event they regard you as an exciting and authoritative source of crucial information, there is a likelihood they will share your content with their numerous followers, hence increasing your audience.

2. The Law of Compounding

The moment you publish high quality content and put effort into creating an online audience with quality followers, they will share the content with their audiences on Facebook, LinkedIn, and even their blogs. Sharing, as well as the discussion of content, creates an opening for various search engines, like Google, to find the content in crucial searches. These entry points may even develop into thousands of possible means for people to find you online.

3. The Law of Value

Don't spend all of your time on social media promoting your services and products; there is the probability that people will quit paying attention to your content. The same applies to excessive live streaming of your brand. This is the reason you should add value to the conversation. Try to focus less on conversions and emphasize fantastic content, as well as creating relationships with other online influencers. Over time, those individuals will become a great catalyst for your business.

4. The Law of Quality

It is quite blatant that quality overrides quantity. It is better to possess two thousand connections online who have read, shared, and made comments on your content, than twenty thousand connections who vanish soon after creating a link with you. It's for this reason that you should ensure the content of your live stream video is of good quality.

5. The Law of Patience

You should keep in mind that success on social media and live streaming, doesn't just happen in one night. It takes takes time - think years, not months - to build a loyal audience. But once you've built that audience, your return on the time and effort it took to grow your platform will be immense.

Chapter 3: What Is Facebook and Why Do You Need to Use It to Grow Your Business or Profile?

Formerly known as 'The Facebook' when it was first launched in 2006, Facebook is a social networking service and is the most visited social media platform in the world with approximately 2.3 billion users worldwide.

Facebook is accessible to anyone with an email address who is above the age of 13. To create an account, visit the Facebook website where you will "sign up" by filling in the necessary information such as your name, age, and gender. Once you have your new account set up, you can personalize your profile and begin to add friends, follow pages, join groups, and create your own posts. Facebook offers its users a convenient and efficient way to stay connected with family, friends, and general news from around the world.

Now, because Facebook has the greatest number of users compared to any other social media network, it is no wonder that brands and publishers are flocking to promote their products through this platform. These users are from all different backgrounds, and it is quite possibly the best platform to use if you are looking to reach a larger customer base.

Creating a business or personal page on Facebook is a way to create exposure for your brand or business. It legitimizes your online presence and helps you engage with customers and followers. You can customize your page or profile by adding information, such as product information, website address, location, contact details, and business hours. You can also send invites to current customers to follow your page or profile. When customers and followers interact with your page, their friends will be able to see this activity on their newsfeed. This is a perfect example of the old marketing strategy, "word of mouth." Another way to gain followers is by promoting your page through competitions or offering a discount code when someone follows your page. A memorable Facebook URL is something to consider as something unique is bound to catch someone's attention.

It is important to make your business page as professional as possible as it is a reflection on the authenticity and capability of your business. With that being said, it is always a good strategy to simply post regularly to keep customers and followers entertained or updated on any new information. Regular photo updates are also a good idea, giving you an opportunity to show off your product or stir up some curiosity about what goes on behind the scenes.

Facebook ads are another option if you wish to reach a wider customer base. There is also 'Facebook Insight,' which is a free and helpful tool that allows you to track relevant information, such as how many times your post has been shared and how many people it has reached.

Engagement, undoubtedly, is the lifeblood of social media and utilizing it in marketing strategies makes Facebook a powerful asset to social media marketing. According to digital marketing expert Brandon Leibowitz, though Facebook doesn't quite have the reach of engagement that Instagram does, "it still has the second highest audience engagement rate among all social networks" (2018).

Facebook ads also perform incredibly well as a marketing tool for businesses. As stated by Social Flow, "Each of the $1.7 billion users is worth $14.17 in annual ad revenue" (Leibowitz, 2018). If you consider how many followers you could garner from Facebook revenue, this social media platform more than provides a means to reach more people.

Facebook has undoubtedly revolutionized social media by creating a free online platform for businesses and brands to socialize with their customers and followers. It has become an essential method of promoting one's business or profile by adding a personal touch to grow a business.

Chapter 4: How to Use Facebook Live

Now that you know why Facebook social media marketing is such a key strategic marketing platform, what next?

Well, the biggest social media sites are continuously improving their services by introducing new and exciting features to foster engagement with clients on the platforms.

Facebook, however, was the first social media website to truly perfect the marketing art of live video. In August 2015, Facebook rolled out Facebook Mentions, later renamed Facebook Live. This feature enabled users to broadcast live video on the app. Since its launch, Facebook Live has quickly risen in popularity. In 2018, it was estimated that approximately 78 percent of online audiences preferred watching videos on Facebook Live than reading content, as live video is more appealing.

Marketers are excited about Facebook Live, all for a good reason. It is a fun and straightforward way to engage with your audience, give critical information about your brand, and gather useful feedback, all in real time. But there are a few nuances to this tool that you will need to know if you want to leverage the power of marketing via Facebook Live:

Quick Guide to Facebook Live Webcam Setup

If you are using a desktop, at the top of your newsfeed, click the icon 'Live Video.' The webcam on your computer will immediately be activated. The procedure in the Facebook mobile app is relatively simple. Click the icon 'Update Status,' then proceed to Facebook Live. You are then required to write a short description of your video before you can start recording it. You can now go ahead and begin your live stream. It really is as simple as that.

Notify Followers When You Plan to Go Live

If you have a massive fan base, it is advisable to always announce when you are going live beforehand. It is one of the best ways to build anticipation and reach more people.

Also, it is well worth cross-promoting your live event on multiple social channels to help maximize your viewership. If you are working with an influencer, it will be even better if they promote the broadcast on their feed, as well. This will help to further increase the number of viewers to your live show.

The more viewers you have, the more your product or service will be promoted. It all comes down to one thing, and that is promoting your business. Without viewers, the entire process is useless, so make sure to announce when you upload a video or live stream to make sure you get those much-coveted views.

Run a Test Launch Beforehand

Test your video before you broadcast it. You can make the post available only to yourself. This will afford you the opportunity to comb through for any errors and check on the quality of your video and audio.

The test run will also help you decide on your objectives. As opposed to just starting a live broadcast and improvising as you go, it is advisable as a marketer to know precisely what you plan on achieving with your broadcast. The test run will give you the viewer's perspective. If you find that you don't like something about the video, chances are, neither will your audience.

To eliminate confusion and the possibility of leaving something out of the broadcast, you can run several test launches until you are satisfied with the results. This will not only focus your conversation on the set objectives, but will also boost your confidence. You will find that with time, you will get better at doing Facebook Live streams and eventually you may do away with test runs altogether.

Introduce Yourself Multiple Times Throughout the Live Stream

You may be tempted to assume that all your fans know who you are, but that is just not the truth. Some of your followers, despite liking your page, don't know you on a personal level. Others are new viewers and friends of current fans who have no idea who you are or what your brand is about.

Since you are the brand, your intention should be to introduce yourself and give a brief description of what your video is about. Not everyone is usually online at the same time. As the video runs, you will get more people joining the broadcast at different stages of the live stream. This is another reason why you should introduce yourself again, along with the purpose of the broadcast. As you notice the number of viewers increasing, keep in mind that if they don't get an incentive to continue watching, they'll stop.

Find the Balance Between Live Streaming and Other Marketing Tools

Facebook Live is a great online marketing tool. Even so, you should not focus all your attention on this single feature. Remember that your audience is different, and although 80 percent prefer watching video, the other 20 percent should also be catered for.

You need to space live videos with another type of content. This strategy will afford you maximum exposure on the platform. However, you have to be savvy about it. For example, since Facebook Live videos rank higher than all other content formats - due to Facebook's algorithm - any important information you need to announce should be done using live streaming video. Why? Because this content format will get the most visibility and reach the largest chunk of your Facebook followers. You can then follow up your message with some other form of content and media.

Don't Let Mistakes and Errors Faze You

Letting mistakes roll off your back is often easier said than done. Even with all the rehearsal in the world, you still might end up making a slip of the tongue on your live stream video. This should not faze you, though. Try to keep in mind that spontaneity, (and yes, that even includes you making the odd mistake) can help lend a sense of authenticity to your brand.

Many things can go wrong once you go live, and the majority of them may not be in your control. Your equipment could suddenly play-up, your internet connection could drop, you may get hit by a wave of nerves, or even momentarily forget what you wanted to say.

This is not a reason for you to stop broadcasting, though! Although such situations may leave you frustrated, you need to learn to adapt and work around them. It shows you are human, and you may even get better engagement with your fans. If you feel like you must correct a mistake or slip-up, do it in such a manner that does not shift focus from the main objective of the video.

Learn how to laugh at yourself, too. It makes you relatable and likable. Since the video is live, your audience will understand that the slip up is just as normal as it would have been if they were standing face-to-face with you. The beauty of Facebook Live is that it is not overly polished. There is only so much scripted content you can put into it. Instead, at some point as your engagement gets more natural and flowing, it will become easier for you to improvise. So, try to joke about any errors if you can, but most importantly, just keep going. Your broadcasts are never going to be perfect, but depending on your attitude, they can effectively pass the message you intend on delivering.

Engage Directly With Your Live Stream Viewers

The best way to naturally increase viewership and engagement is by actively interacting with your audience. Since you are live, it is imperative that after introductions you give a breakdown of what you plan on talking about. Let your audience know what you expect from them. If you expect questions or any form of engagement, let them know beforehand.

Facebook Live gives you the opportunity to not only instantly respond to questions, but you can also use a different device for replying to questions in the live stream's chat box - all of which allows you to engage in direct audience conversations in real time.

What's more, is that the more comments your live stream gets, the higher your live stream video's relevancy score will be. This, in turn, determines how high you will rank on the user's Facebook feed.

One trick for encouraging more audience interaction is to mention individual audience members by name (especially when they ask you a question in the chatbox). This strategy not only makes your audience feel honored, but also generates a sense of intimacy between you and them. It is important to call someone by their name since it makes them feel special and appreciated. Such a fan will most definitely share the broadcast, like, and comment on it.

With time, you will have some fans who will make multiple appearances in your broadcasts. Always make sure to shout them out every once in a while. Since a live stream can still be viewed long after the broadcast has ended, make sure to go back and respond to any comments that may have been dropped after your video. Don't leave any questions unanswered. In fact, the best result for your live stream video chat responses would be for your live video stream to spark an ongoing conversation within your audience. This will go a long way towards cultivating a real culture for the community, making everyone feel included and involved with your brand.

Also, don't forget you're as human as they come. You do not have to be perfect. Be yourself, and you will realize that your little quirks are what make you more relatable to your followers.

Share Your Live Stream Broadcast Link on Other Platforms

When you are done recording, share the broadcast on the different pages you manage, in groups, to your profile, and email the link to your subscribers. Additionally, you can add the broadcast to your website.

This will draw more people to your Facebook page and encourage multiple views. You need to create a personal touch with your audience for this to work. There is a fine line between interesting content and downright spam. This is why you need to be personable and authentic. The internet is already full of touched-up videos and photoshopped images. Believe it or not, people don't want to see perfection.

You want to be honest, open, and as human as possible. This one-on-one connection with your audience will give you the edge you need to improve your brand.

Fashion Your Broadcast Like a Story

Videos should have an outline similar to a simple story; there should be a beginning, a middle, and an end.

Think of some attention-grabbing tidbits ahead of time, and use them at the beginning of your live stream in order to actively keep your audience engaged before you get right into the meat and bones of your show. For example, you could open with a personal story about yourself and the brand, expand on a key industry statistic and how it ties into your business, or tell a few fun facts to entertain your viewers. In other words, you need to start your broadcasts with high energy and connect with your audience from the get-go.

While the middle of your broadcast is where you tell the bulk of your story, keep in mind that your audience will join your live stream at different points of broadcast. Because of this, make sure you reintroduce the topic and any live guests periodically through the stream. These reintroduction breaks are also a good place to encourage the audience to participate and "comment in the chat box below."

The last key component of your broadcast is the ending. Keep in mind what your objectives were to begin with. Remind yourself of what you expect your audience's next move to be. Summarize the important take away first, thank your guests for joining you (if you had an interview session), and show appreciation to your fans for participating, as well. Remind your audience of what they should take away from the session, and reiterate this in the comments section.

After finishing your live stream, the next step should not be about when to host the next show. You need to first look at the work you have done and analyze it for any tips you might use for next time. Evaluate what did not work, what could have worked, and what should have been removed entirely. The next time you post a live stream, incorporate what you've learned from the last live stream in order to make the next session even better.

In addition to focusing on how you performed, you should view the comments sections and see what reaction your audience had in regards to the broadcast. This will help you evaluate what your audience responded to most and what they didn't like at all.

To step up your game even further, look at how your competitors are using Facebook Live to grow their businesses. Performing a similar analysis as you do on your live videos will give you a sense of what works for the audience. This is easy to do since you and your competitors most likely have the same audience type. Learn their tactics and the topics they engage in that seem to resonate more with the fans. As the demand for video consumption continues to rise in online social media platforms, it is predicted that Facebook Live will grow even more in popularity. Creating great content for your live streams is not as hard as it may seem at first. With an open mind and a resilient spirit, you, too, will find Facebook Live to be a great tool in your social media marketing arsenal.

Chapter 5: What Is YouTube and Why Do You Need to Use It to Grow Your Business or Profile?

YouTube is an online video sharing website that was first launched in 2005. It allows users to upload video content and in turn, users can rate, comment, like, and share these videos.

YouTube users can subscribe to different YouTube channels which will allow them immediate access to all videos from their subscribed channels and to receive notifications when a new video is uploaded. The majority of YouTube videos are free to view, and many different forms of promotions and adverts are used on this platform. YouTube is the second most popular website used in the world, after Google, and before Facebook.

YouTube receives over a billion visitors on their site monthly. With such a large amount of people browsing videos, it offers many opportunities to grow your business or profile. It also has an easy video sharing option which makes it possible to spread your uploaded content. You can attach your video links from YouTube to your other social media accounts, instead of having to upload a video on each separate website. With the option of liking and disliking videos, you will be able to see the positive and negative responses to your content. At first, it may seem like a daunting task to use videos to grow your business, but with enough motivation and patience, you will be well on your way.

Across the world, there are about 1.325 billion YouTube users. Every second, five hours of video is uploaded to this platform. This high number of users explains why YouTube marketing is quickly becoming a major marketing tool for businesses. For example, for the past few years, Cisco - an IT and networking hardware conglomerate - has been focused on improving their routers, since the amount of web traffic caused by video content has risen exponentially. In fact, as of 2018, it is estimated that 78 percent of the internet's content is now video-based.

This illustrates the importance of video in marketing. Quite often, a video as simple as a product review can garner massive numbers of views, especially if the product marketed is innovative and the reviewer is well-known.

The growth in popularity of online live streaming has risen immensely over the past two years. For instance, the number of viewers in 2017 was 81 percent higher than the viewers in 2016. What's more, this trend is expected to continue. Researchers have predicted that by 2021, the entire live video streaming industry will be worth more than $70 billion.

The most recent upgrade for live streaming is the live streaming mobile apps. Even though it launched just last year, it has gained a lot of popularity among selected android users. By 2016, the publicly-available YouTube videos with over 25,000 views became 2.8 billion. The number increased to 6.9 billion, which was 200 percent by 2017. These numbers and statistics do not lie; the web is now turning to video. YouTube marketing is the way to go for both offline and online business owners. Taking advantage of this shift in web content is important.

There is no better time to trial-run YouTube Live for the marketing of your brand than now. Do not dive into this blindly, though. Mistakes are bound to happen, which may cost your brand's image big time. Being cautious and learning the best practices from professionals will help kick-start your business for your YouTube marketing plan. It is essential to stay on top of all features and upgrades on YouTube if you want to consistently achieve the most out of every live stream session. Besides, YouTube Live offers more services than you may be aware of.

One example of this would be YouTube Sponsorships. YouTube Sponsorships are basically a partnership between two brands in an attempt to promote one another. Larger brands may be paid to collaborate, while smaller ones only aim to get more exposure and gain followers. You may be given a link to place in your video to direct viewers to the collaborating brand's website, or be sent products to review on a stream. Quality content is of enormous importance to sponsors, so always aim to give your all in a stream in order to attract sponsorships.

A Quick Primer on the History of YouTube Live

Over the years, YouTube Live has changed a lot. So how did this platform originally develop?

Well, as early as 2010, Google had already begun broadcasting popular events online. Famous musical concerts and political events, like President Obama's press conferences, were among the first events to be broadcasted on YouTube Live. Later, they began testing a live feature on their platform with selected users across the world. Success with these few users had the company open the doors for everyone to use this platform.

On which platforms can you find YouTube Live streaming? YouTube Live is available on three different platforms:

1. YouTube.com

2. YouTube Gaming

3. YouTube mobile app

All three platforms offer essentially the same service. Once you stream a live video, it is automatically saved for your viewers to watch at a later time. All three platforms also give the content's owner the right to protect their content through the YouTube Content ID system. It allows you to choose whether you will release your content to the public for free or for a fee (via YouTube's paid content streaming service).

Differences Between YouTube's Three Streaming Platforms

Just a few differences separate the three platforms.

For instance, with the desktop version and the mobile app version, the setup is slightly different.

With the gaming platform and titular site, users are at liberty to create immediate streaming. This platform gives up to 12 hours of video for public consumption.

The choice of saving the content will depend on the owner; you can choose to either save or discard your video content.

All three platforms have the 'Events' feature. You are given a maximum of eight hours to record such events.

Chapter 6: How to Use YouTube Live

The process of recording a live event on the YouTube Live platform is a little different. Look for 'Go Live' in the YouTube channel section of your YouTube account; you will need to enter a title before going on to fill in a form.

In the past, only users with more than 10 thousand subscribers were allowed to use this particular feature. However, that number has since been lowered to just one thousand subscribers. This has allowed the feature to become available for most people since getting one thousand subscribers is relatively achievable for most new channels.

Now, once you are ready to go live, here are some of the best practices for making sure your YouTube live session goes off without a hitch:

Video Sequence

To make sure you get your timing down, try to ensure your sequencing is perfect. Viewers easily get bored with long video content (i.e. any video over 10 to 15 minutes long), so to ensure maximum viewership, make your content at most five minutes long. Marketing video is different from ordinary YouTube video, and there are some important factors to take into consideration when making a live stream video intended for brand promotion.

First, inform the viewer of who you are or what your product is all about. Here, do not give too much information. Leave the viewers curious. Too much information will easily scare away viewers because of the negative perception of your product. Also, inform the viewer of any other platforms they can find you. In the case of a technicality or networking problem when viewing the content, they then have an alternative platform to find your content on.

Tell Them What to Expect

After the brief introduction, give some information about your video. The information needed here includes why they should watch the video - basically why the viewer is expected to benefit from watching the video. More important information you should give your viewers is the length of your video. As I have mentioned, a long, stretched out video is likely to cause the loss of viewers. This is one of the most important factors in determining if your viewers will continue to watch, or exit out of it. Having a short video will make the viewers feel as if they won't waste too much time, so it's okay to watch the entire thing. If they see other recommended videos of yours around the same length, they'll watch those, too.

Give Them the Real Information

Without making your viewer impatient, deliver your message in the clearest and simplest way. Ensure your message is easily understandable for your viewers. This is the make-or-break moment for your viewers. At this point, they will judge whether their time was well spent or a waste of time. Consult widely before coming up with this message. Look at success stories and borrow their ideas. Alternatively, seek help from an information strategist. If you feel you are not well placed to deliver the message, let someone you believe is better than you vocally to deliver the message.

Here's a recap:

Remind the viewer what information you are giving, briefly. Ensure that this part is as short as possible. Otherwise, you will risk making your viewers bored with your video.

Humor is key. While giving your information, excite your viewers with humorous information related to your original message. This could be advice, warnings, or recommendations. Through this piece, you will remove the viewer's perception that you are only interested in selling your product. It is essential for your viewers to feel as if you care about their well-being. This part of your video could change everything if delivered well. Be as honest as possible.

Call to Action

You did not produce your video for fun. How can it improve your brand? Many YouTube video-makers miss this part; your video should have a CTA asking viewers to subscribe to your channel or buy something before watching more videos. As you near the end of your video, take a moment to show your viewers the link they have to follow in order to find more information on your product. People enjoy clicking on things and following links. Whether it's out of curiosity or genuine interest, it really doesn't matter because you are getting clicks and your product or service is getting exposed. It's basic human nature to want to push buttons or click on things. Exploit that.

Video Creation

During the initial stages of creating your YouTube channel, this is a problem you are likely to experience. Not everyone will be excited with the idea of appearing on YouTube. The beauty of YouTube Live streaming is you can use others to spread your message. Many people use celebrities, like athletes or musicians, to promote their products. Even though this venture could be expensive, it has proven to bear more fruit than using ordinary people. You may also gain a larger audience through collaborating with various individuals who already have an online presence. It may be difficult to come up with original content, but bringing something new to the table is bound to gain you some attention. Adding to this, here are some tricks to remember when making content:

Don't draw things out. It is better to keep something short and simple rather than possibly boring your audience. Make sure the first few seconds are interesting enough to keep them watching more.

Your content should be memorable and something worth talking about. A specific topic should be presented, leaving a bold statement and encouraging individuals to spread your content through discussion.

Make it possible to use a video for multiple purposes such as promoting an upcoming event, a new product, or your other social media accounts.

Different contents are proposed to achieve different goals. Here is a list of what your video content is intended to accomplish:

Make Sales Directly

This is the simplest way to increase your sales. When your primary goal is to make sales, your message is simple and should include the price of your product, where your product is found, and how you can place an order. This applies whenever there is a promotion or offer for new customers. What is it that will excite your customers the most?

Build Your Brand's Website

If your long term goal is to increase the popularity of your site, you have to trust in your course of action and do it without hesitation. It is difficult to quantify your progress here. Patience is key. Do it well, and for a long period, and you will see that the popularity of your website will increase over time. Once you have a solid customer base, the rest will follow. Loyal subscribers, clients, and people who often buy your products will be sure to share your videos and links if the content and products or services are entertaining and good enough.

Build the Readership of Your Website

Through your live stream video, explain to your viewers why they should check out your website; why it is unique and what will your viewers gain from going through your site? Through YouTube Live, you might get direct sales or direct subscribers for your website.

Find a Lead

In your video, ask viewers to click the link to your website. Explain to them the value of clicking the link. Ensure you track customers who click on your link. Ask them if they have questions. A prompt and helpful solution will increase your customer relations.

Tips for Success in YouTube Live Stream Marketing

Quality Is Key

Never compromise the quality of your content. Always ensure your video is both audibly and visually up to standard. Don't make your viewers struggle in watching your video. This refers to what I've said earlier. It is always better to spend a bit more than to compromise the quality of the video. Wherever possible, stream from interesting locations with good lighting or somewhere with an aesthetically pleasing background. It might cost a little more, but the content is worth it. Make your viewers' experience as enjoyable as possible. All this starts with the quality of your device. A good device can provide clarity for your content.

Early Promotion

This can be provided by a feature such as the 'Events' option. Through this, you will be able to get your viewers excited about seeing your video. You can also utilize platforms, such as email, to communicate to the public about an upcoming live stream event. The most commonly used ways to give a snippet on a future event is the use of a trailer. This is a short video showing the viewers what they can expect to see in the full version.

Use the Right Equipment

Your effort is not enough to provide a quality video. The device used matters a lot. Can your device handle a large volume of broadcasting? What clarity does your device offer? Here are some essential factors you should consider:

- Finding a reliable internet connection

- Your encoder should be dedicated

- Having a computer with high capacity

- Plan out a backup option

- Utilize a quality webcam and microphone

Do a Necessary Test Ahead of the Real Thing

Before starting your live stream, test all your equipment to ensure that it's working well. Do this 24 hours before the actual event. This will allow time to replace or rectify a faulty device. If everything is okay, do the same 30 minutes before the event.

Monitor the Feedback

During the live stream, viewers will probably give feedback such as to move your microphone closer to your mouth, or to set your camera correctly. This feedback will improve the quality of your video. Also, there is nothing more annoying than a streamer who squints while reading comments from the chat box. This is why a big chat box is important. This will allow you to read the comments quickly and effectively without irritating your viewers.

What Is Your Plan B?

If things go wrong during the message delivery, will you stop your video? If you experience a blackout, what happens? Have a standby laptop. The worst thing you can do during a live stream event is shut down without an explanation. This will discredit the viewer's perception of your message. This is where the other platforms come in handy, too. Also, make sure you have a backup plan in case the wifi is down. Always, *always* have a plan B.

Chapter 7: What Is Instagram and Why Do You Need to Use It to Grow Your Business or Profile?

Instagram is among the most popular social media platforms today. You should consider marketing your business using this platform, if you haven't already done so. Instagram keeps improving their services to help companies succeed in their marketing. One of these features is Instagram Live. Introduced in November 2016, this feature enables users to post videos throughout the day for their followers to view.

A whopping 100 million Instagram users post and watch live every single day. If this is not incentive enough for you to use Instagram for live marketing, I don't know what is. Businesses can effectively use Instagram Live to connect and engage with their customers, provided you remain true to your brand.

As we've mentioned above, Facebook is an extremely helpful social media platform to get you started on your marketing journey, but Instagram is the key to live stream product placement. Instagram has users located all over the world, which means the overall diversity of your clientele will increase dramatically through using this tool. Perhaps this is why Instagram is rated number one on the list of social media platforms likely to provide the most reach (Leibowitz, 2018).

Like all social media platforms, Instagram provides a cheaper way to initiate marketing tools. When looking for a younger audience, Instagram is the key (Leibowitz, 2018). Most users are also familiar with live streaming, which is where marketers tend to gain helpful feedback for their products and services.

Because Instagram largely depends on images, visual aspects of the platform are especially important. This is why live videos on Instagram tend to work out well. Exciting and innovative ideas tend to take off on the site, and even elegantly written words provide excellent bases for future work.

Instagram Stories

This is among the most popular feature on the platform. Instagram stories have a lifespan of just 24 hours after they are posted. You can post photos, recorded videos, plain text, and boomerangs. These can be accompanied by hashtags, stickers, location tags, and temperature.

Interaction with your fan base is made even easier using the stickers for polls, sliding bars, and questions. You can furthermore leverage the question feature and host a weekly 'ask me anything' feature, where you get to tackle common questions about your brand. Story highlights are another fun way to draw positive attention to your brand. Until you get rid of them, they will stay in your profile.

The short-lived nature of Instagram stories provides an excellent pull for current and future consumers. Because the stories are only available for a day, promotional videos featuring giveaways and additional rewards are especially vital for increasing consumer growth. When customers only have a short time to input information or use your hashtag, many are likely to visit your site in higher volumes.

Live Videos

Beside Instagram stories, you can take advantage of streaming live videos to give your audience a look into the behind-the-scenes aspect of your brand. This can be leveraged to advertise new arrivals, boost sales of existing ones, and answer live questions through comments.

The videos last only for 24 hours, but if you want it to stay on your feed longer, you can upload content shot directly through the app to post.

Presently, Instagram Live remains unparalleled in its ability to connect businesses to their fan base. As the newest addition to Instagram, this feature puts you directly in touch with your audience, thereby generating a genuine and more intimate experience in comparison to other forms of content.

Instagram Live has some rewards attached to it as incentive to drive users to use the feature more. This is a plus if you want to reach your audience through this platform. Instagram has made it a step easier for you by providing a few bonuses:

Priority in the feed. Instagram Live puts you at the front and center of your audience feed. The Instagram algorithm will ensure that your live video will appear at the top of users' news feeds, increasing the chances of your post being seen.

Fan notification. Don't be worried about going live without your followers being aware of it. Send the notification reminder to all of your followers immediately before you start broadcasting. This feature is on by default, so you don't need to turn on notifications to be alerted. Through this, you will have peace of mind since your live video will be broadcast as widely as possible.

Post-broadcast boosts. This addition is relatively new to Instagram Live. It allows your followers to continue watching your video within 24 hours of posting it. The video will still indicate that it is live on people's feed, making it even easier to engage with them for longer.

Chapter 8: How to Use Instagram Live Live Stream As a Marketing Strategy on Instagram

While using the live video as a medium to pass your message, you need to hit the spot between spontaneity and professionalism. Although the whole point of live streaming is to eliminate the feel of post-production editing, your videos need to revolve around a focal point. You need to come up with a central topic that you will highlight during the session.

Promote your Instagram Live on your Instagram stories. Let your followers know you will soon be going live. Be specific on the exact time and topics you wish to cover. Additionally, this is an opportunity to let them know what you expect from them as far as engagement is concerned. Since not all your followers are in the same time-zone, be sure to add this little detail on your promotional Instagram stories.

The more buzz you create beforehand, the more viewers you can attract. If you want to launch a product, use this opportunity to give a sneak peek of what you're planning to release. A little teasing will go a long way in getting your audience vamped up for the live video.

While your live video still gets massive viewership after you have posted it, it will serve you best if you can get the majority during the actual stream. This will increase engagement and make the chat room even livelier with comments streaming in real time. Such a scenario can spark a conversation between your followers that you can join in. This kind of one-on-one engagement is not easy to get after your live video ends.

Promoting your Instagram Live video should not just be limited to Instagram stories. You should go all out to try and reach as many of your followers as possible. Send a newsletter to your email list. One email should be sent a few days before you go live, and the other just before you start broadcasting. This will inform your fans beforehand about the event and remind them about it just before you go live.

Aside from Instagram stories, you can leverage other options on the platform for this purpose. Post a photo to announce your upcoming event on your story. Although it might seem crazy, doing a live video to announce when you plan on going live works. Create hashtags for your consumers and new consumers to share. Creating keywords for your products and services gives them a standing on search engines, as well. Many businesses who promote using these hashtags show up on top spots on SEO.

You probably have a host of accounts on other social media platforms. Use sites like Facebook and Twitter to create a buzz about your upcoming event. Your website should also sing the same song. Although it might not necessarily get you many viewers, you have to try everything in order to maximize attendance. You will want to blast these sites with news of your intention to go live to garner as many viewers as you possibly can on the actual day. That being said, there are a few tips you can use to maximize the effect of your live video.

Host a Pre-Show

Hosting a pre-show is a good idea depending on what you want to talk about. This is important because if a follower catches your live video somewhere in the middle, they will stop watching if they can't keep up with what you are talking about. This is why a pre-show briefly highlighting the details of your live show is a great idea. The pre-show should last about five minutes, which is enough time for people to come on board.

Define Your Goals

Although this is not necessary, you should go into your live video with a clear mindset of what you want to achieve. This gives you focus on what to talk about and how best to engage your audience.

Whether it is driving sales, promoting a specific product, or just fighting with your fans, having a set goal will give you a yardstick with which to measure your performance later. Even though Instagram Live is not the best way to drive sales, it is a strong feature for building your brand and creating a robust customer-brand engagement. You can further entice the audience by sharing an exclusive discount with your live attendees. This will foster a feeling of exclusivity and can help drive your sales. You need to be creative in coming up with a timely ask for this at the end of your video.

Your goal should contain an outline of the points you want to drive home. There's nothing worse than a live video that just doesn't seem to end. Such a video goes on and on and, at some point, starts repeating already highlighted points.

Your outline shouldn't confine you, though, and it goes without saying that specificity will get you results. Even when you do go off script, ensure that whatever you say or add is in tandem with the topic of the day. Don't be afraid to go 'off script' from time to time. Often, this is usually the highlight of the video and makes for a memorable moment.

Be Engaging

Maintain a high tempo on your video. Since you will be interacting live with your audience, their time is invaluable. As a result, you do not want to bore them with a conversation that starts out great, but tapers off toward the end. Start, remain, and finish on a high tempo.

It is your responsibility to keep the interaction and chat room alive. Communicating in a bland monotone voice will lose your audience's attention. The key factor here is to engage and interact with viewers you already have.

If a fan says, "Hi," reply to the greeting. Answer all questions to the best of your knowledge. Remember, you are here for the audience.

People associate a brand with its employees. Your interaction with the audience will either sell your business, or lose it. A bad experience is enough to put a fan off, and an unsatisfied customer is a dangerous entity for the business. Smile often, and foster a cheerful mood. Thankfully, there are face filters you can use to add extra fun to your video.

To reduce monotony, you should consider hosting a Q&A session with your audience. The topic for your video could merely be answering questions and tackling any challenges the audience may have with your product or service. It is a vital way of strengthening the relationship between brand and client, as well as helping people better understand your brand. You may find that such a session would receive better hits than one aimed at selling a certain product to your audience. Often, customers have many reservations about companies that focus solely on sales minus customer needs.

All in all, don't let any of your audience members leave the chat room unsatisfied. This is fodder for a bad review, and you just cannot afford such publicity, especially online. Ensure that you convince them to buy your brand, as well as your loyalty.

Record High-Quality Videos

When watching a video, 67 percent of online users perceive video quality as the most important feature. Similarly, according to a live stream survey, 23 percent would not confidently purchase from a brand that posted a poor quality video.

Quality matters. It means someone was thoughtful enough to look into the details. A poor quality video just shows you do not care enough about your brand or your audience's experience. As a result, you risk losing the fans you already have and missing out on hundreds you could have potentially gained.

While filming, invest in a good quality phone and ensure that your wifi connection is great. This goes for your service reception, too. Any hiccups in live streaming can deter viewers from watching your show. The sad reality is, no one is patient enough to stick around while you sort out your connection. They just leave. Period.

Highlight Day-to-Day Operations and Events

Eighty-seven percent of people prefer to watch behind-the-scenes content online. Whether your company is hosting an event or attending a summit, share this with your online audience. Posting still photos of the event is not enough to give them the full feel of the experience.

Let's say your company is hosting the local community at your office. Rather than confine the forum to the physical audience in the room, live stream the event to give your online audience a raw, behind-the-scenes experience. You should have a team member manage the online audience who can similarly participate in the forum, ask questions, and learn just as much as the rest.

This is not only a fun experience for all attendees, but it goes to show just how invested you are in your brand. People stick to a brand because they like the experience they get from the team. Ever wondered why people love watching behind-the-scenes footage of movie sets? It's because enjoying a movie is not enough. The full experience comes in knowing what happens where the camera doesn't reach. Knowing what celebrities are like when they are not shooting - these are usually the best clips. The same applies to your brand.

Most of the time, one product is usually not much different from the next. The true sign of power is if people choose you over everyone else. This is why you need your audience to connect with the people behind the brand.

You need to train your team in how to behave and speak for the brand. If you get your team as invested in the brand as you are, you shouldn't have any problems with your business. Many times we have seen customers swear off a product because an employee spoke ill of the company. Whether the negative publicity is true or false does little to repair the broken trust.

People buy because they have connected with someone on the inside. Your audience wants to know the vibe of your company, what the people are like, and what they think about the company themselves. Then, for a situation where you have multiple people representing your brand, take care to instill in them the principles you want to be reflected to the world.

Endorse, Launch, and Use a Product

Use Instagram Live as a platform to promote a new product. Announce to your followers the expected date of the launch in a video and talk the product up. Honestly, this is the best place for a tease or live launch. Explain to your customers what makes your product stand out from the competitors'.

Create a buzz beforehand and go live a few minutes before the official launch, involving your audience in raw footage of the product launch. The suspense your video builds will draw your audiences to stick to the whole video until the very end. This is a popular tactic Apple has successfully exploited.

Release a few details concerning the product in question, leaving the viewers in more suspense than they would care to admit. Done the right way, this tease will drum up your viewership and boost sales. Afterward, be sure to encourage them to buy your product, leaving accurate information about the price and where to find it. This will ultimately boost sales and customer acceptance for your new product.

Aside from promotions, another recent trend Instagram live has seen is videos demonstrating how to use a particular product. Timing product demonstrations with the product launch is a great way to get a good head start. Make sure the product you're launching is available to the public at the time your video goes live.

It is not enough to just hype a product and then leave the audience to their own devices. Showing them how to use the product, no matter how easy, is a great show of trust and care on your part. Say you run a makeup company; Live streaming tutorials on how to effectively apply the makeup, while giving tips on what shades match best with different skin tones, would mean a huge boost in your sales. Even though these things may seem trivial, they have a great impact on how your audience views your brand.

Host an Influencer

Doing a live stream with an influencer is an excellent way to vamp up your viewership and, ultimately, sales. To provide an expert opinion on the topic you are dealing with, you need to feature an influencer in a similar industry. Also, get an influencer your audience looks up to.

The good thing about this is that influencers usually have a mass online following of their own. During the hype up leading to your live event, it is advisable to have the influencer with you to give a sneak peek of what the two of you will be discussing. Additionally, the influencer will invite his or her audience, guaranteeing you massive video viewership. The takeaway here is not only will you build a strong case for your brand, but your followers will also increase tenfold and the influencer's presence will drive up your sales.

If you are a clothing store, for example, teaming up with a young and popular fashion model could be a great boost for your business. The model could spot your articles, and the two of you could discuss how to pair colors and fabrics for different seasons and weather.

If the influencer you're targeting is not in the same location as you, Instagram has you covered. With a new feature called collab-live stream, you and your influencer could both host a live stream at different locations at the same time. There is no limit to online marketing.

If you want to reap some benefits for your live marketing campaign, assemble a special offer for the attendees. This is a great incentive for them to come back next time, possibly with their friends. Offer a coupon or discount for your product, specifically to your live audience. The special offer will get people spending on your products; even those who don't need what you're offering may know someone who does. This is how you build a strong fan base.

Building your brand doesn't necessarily increase the number of people viewing your posts and watching your videos. The numbers do not work that way. Your brand image encompasses who you are, your opinion on the matters people care about, and why they should trust you over a competitor.

This is why getting your audience to first trust you is imperative. If they trust you, they will be interested in you, and they will buy your brand. The best thing about building a solid brand reputation is that it resonates within generations. People influence their families, friends, and co-workers. This human connection your audience has outside social media is going to be the driving force that will keep you afloat long after your message has been forgotten.

Many households stick to a brand of soap or read the same newspaper for most of their lives. Research suggests that adults are most likely going to buy the same products they used in their homes as children, even after they move out to start their own families. This is the power of branding. Aim at fostering trust with your audience, and you can be assured a lasting business.

Chapter 9: What Is Twitch and Why Do You Need to Use It to Grow Your Business or Profile?

Twitch Live Streaming Marketing

Twitch is a video streaming platform owned by Amazon. It's the biggest destination for video games. If you are a fan of video games, chances that you have stumbled upon this platform are high. In one month, the number of Twitch Live viewers hit up to 140 million views. However, of all these visitors, two million of them spend over two hours streaming videos per day. Twitch Live streaming is not one of the most popular social media channels among marketers, but what you need to understand is that digital marketing is not always about running your advertisements on the most popular channels.

Quite likely, Twitch is one of the best social media marketing platforms you've never heard of. If you're a gamer, it's likely that you've at least heard about it. Since Amazon is gaining popularity in online consumption, Twitch allows consumers to play developed games and, best of all, they are niche-specific (Laubscher, 2018). This means that if you are marketing your brand to a specific type of customer or customer base, Twitch provides the means to narrow your search. This ad reaches those who look for specific things.

Loyal Twitch users also get perks they would not have received if they had bought from another site (Laubscher, 2018). These prizes are specific to Twitch - such as obtaining a Twitch Crate - that encourage people to invest in this growing site.

Again, we have mentioned that Twitch is not the most common site for ordinary consumption, but it is growing rapidly. Amazon has also just recently opened the door to additional marketing ads on its site, so becoming a marketer early may land you a prime spot on the long list of marketers likely to soon become affiliated with the site.

According to Amazon, the large team wants to create a closer community with its users, so Twitch is essential for achieving their goal. For the vast majority of Prime users, Twitch offers merchandise to these members, which makes becoming part of the community enticing.

Setting Up a Twitch Account

The first thing you need to do is set up a broadcasting app on your device. You can install this app using open broadcaster software. The broadcaster software is available on Mac, XSplit, Linux, and even Windows. While some, like OBS, have free access, XSplit has a subscription fee for obtaining improved features.

After setting up an account, set up a new account or log in using your Twitch.tv. At the right side of your screen on the drop-down menu, select Dashboard. Here, go to the playing tab and select a game you want to play before entering the broadcast's title. Since you're looking to configure this platform for live streaming, right-click the OBS, then Run Administrator. On the streaming devices section, select Twitch as your choice. When you are here, return to the dashboard and select Stream Key. A streaming code will be sent. Copy and paste the code to the stream key box and select OK.

Twitch Live streaming also allows you to live stream from your mobile device through the camera. The first thing you need to do here is set up a profile by tapping on the camera button on the right side of your status. Through this device, you can stream your day-to-day activities through your mobile device.

Making Money Through Twitch Streaming

Although Twitch Live streaming is a free service, there are ways you can make money through this platform. Users will be charged a fee under two circumstances. First, when a user subscribes, and, secondly, when the user no longer wants to see pop-up advertisements. Twitch has three subscription packages: $4.99, $9.99, and $24.99, charged every month. All three packages come with different features. As a user, read all package inclusions and decide which one best suits you.

Bits - On the flipside, as a user, you can also earn money through this platform. There are donations known as 'bits' which, by accepting these donations from users, you can earn money from.

eSport - Gamers often arrange games against each other. The winners of these competitions will take home various prizes.

Influencer - This is probably the most lucrative way of making money through Twitch, by launching a career. The most popular way is Twitch Streamer Ninja.

Chapter 10: How to Use Twitch Live

The first thing you need to do is choose whether you want to become a Twitch partner or identify your Twitch partner. There are marketing benefits to becoming a member. According to the Twitch website, by becoming a member, you will receive:

- Channel subscriptions

- Bits

- Ads

If you're unfamiliar with bits, now is the best time to learn. Bits are "a virtual good viewers can buy to Cheer on your channel, allowing them to support you without leaving Twitch." According to the Twitch Partner Program, "Twitch provides participating Partners a share of the revenue Twitch receives from Bits equal to 1 cent per Bit used to Cheer for them" (2019). Bits are extremely important to gaining access to Twitch's partner deal.

Here are several ways you can become a Twitch partner:

- Have a schedule to broadcast regularly for at least three weeks.

- Establish a good audience that will actively chat on your platform.

- Ensure you adhere to the rules and regulations of Twitch.

As a Twitch partner, some of the priorities you are offered include running post-roll ads, pre-roll ads, and mid-roll ads. To ensure your brand gets maximum viewership, go for streamers with a large following number. Every eight minutes, they run commercial ads on their platform. Research done by a marketing company found that 82 percent of users on Twitch are satisfied with their services. They recognize the hospitable environment offered to marketers by this platform.

Examples of brands That Are Already Making It Big Through Twitch Live

Even though Twitch marketing is a relatively new platform in the marketing industry, many industries are already making it big. Here are examples of sectors making it through Twitch marketing:

EA

EA partnered with the Sims 4 Twitch Streaming company to promote the Cats & Dogs industry promoting the products of this company. The two hours of streaming proved to be a success since viewers were given a chance to discuss the various features of this product. All the positives of these products were discussed during the live event. Generally, the ad positioned this product as generous in the eyes of the viewers.

KFC

To advertise its product, the fast-food chain company joined hands with Twitch Streamer Lupo for promotions. KFC offered fast food as the prize for winners of the game. This marketing strategy worked well for both companies. KFC's popularity grew immensely among gamers. Not only that, but the promotions also attracted many new players.

Duracell

In a five-hour streaming broadcast, Duracell used an influencer's Twitch account to broadcast and promote its product. The promotion involved 25 different challenges to prove the strength of a new Duracell battery. The development became a success as it had 187 thousand views and a total of 355 thousand minutes watched. In addition to that, the five-hour video had 480 thousand interactions.

Influencer Marketing on Twitch

When you think of the word "influencer marketing," you should be thinking about the popular marketing platforms such as YouTube, Facebook, and Instagram. The last marketing platform you will probably think of is Twitch Marketing. A huge advantage that Twitch Marketing offers you is the chance to interact with a particular audience.

Initially, Twitch was created specifically for online gaming. This, however, has changed over time and Twitch has expanded its range of activities. This online platform came to be in 2011, and its popularity attracted Amazon enough for them to buy the app in 2014. They say numbers don't lie. By the end of 2016, this platform had 241 billion minutes of gaming content.

There are two ways you can stream content on Twitch. One is through the Twitch website, and the other is through an app. Apps are available for Androids and iOS. Twitch apps are also available for Xbox 360, Xbox One, Amazon's Fire TV, Google Chromecast, and Roku.

Marketers ought to understand the official ages for Twitch gamers. Kids under the age of 13 are not allowed to use this platform. Statistics show that most Twitch users are between the ages of 18 and 49. In terms of gender, only 25 percent of Twitch users are women. It is important for marketers to be aware of these statistics before choosing which products to advertise on Twitch.

Many companies have realized that the uses of traditional advertising methods are no longer bearing fruit. They have acknowledged the influence gamers with a huge following can have. Marketers refer to these kinds of gamers as influencers, as well. When you are targeting an ordinary Twitch user, the most appropriate method is influencer marketing.

Influencers are experienced gamers with many followers. Gaming companies give some influencers advertising space. They play a crucial role in promoting upcoming games. Besides supporting upcoming games, influencers also have plenty of space below their page to advertise various other products. During a live event, gamers are not prohibited from talking about products of their choice. The most appropriate products to advertise on this platform are youth-oriented products, such as pizza and Coca-Cola.

Influencers have built a sizable following on Twitch. Various articles have listed the most influential gamers on Twitch. Choose one gamer with a sizable following and sponsor his channel.

Alternatively, the logo of your brand could appear on the influencer's page for a given period. This will depend on the amount of money you are willing to pay the influencer. Many gamers will visit their 'celebrity' page, possibly seeing the logo of your brand. Many people will trust whatever their celebrities approve of, and this is true even in day-to-day life.

As a marketer, it is important to narrow down your choices according to the product you are advertising. A perfect example is the case of Nike. This company advertises its products on sport-related games on Twitch since players of these games are more likely to be interested in these types of products. Statistics show that 70 percent of gamers who love playing soccer games actually play it in real life. It is practical for companies like Nike to promote their products on sports games.

Conclusion

As a final thought, here are the various ways of successfully using live streaming for marketing.

The concept of social media marketing and live streaming is one of the major contemporary issues attributed to the internet, but more so to social media. Having read this book, you have learned how the four major live streaming platforms can help in taking your brand to the next level. By means of summarizing, I will take you through the three most important things we have learned about each of the live streaming platforms.

Facebook viewers prefer live stream over recorded videos. Research has shown that Facebook users spend more time watching live stream videos compared to recorded video. Live streaming video is more exciting to viewers than recorded content or news feeds. Therefore, marketers should consider marketing their products through live streaming.

Judge the performance of your live video by the number of viewers watching live. In this book, I have told you of the various ways of promoting your video after the live video. You can promote your videos through platforms, such as blogs, and through emails and other social media platforms. After a promotional campaign, you will realize that your video will have dozens of viewers and shares per day. It is important to learn that the process of live streaming should not stop at the end of the broadcast.

Gestures are important during Facebook live streaming. Interestingly enough, on average, 85 percent of live stream viewers on Facebook watch videos without sound. People log in to Facebook in places with a large number of people. As a marketer, ensure your video is as interesting as possible.

When using Instagram, setting goals are important. Before kicking off your Instagram live streaming video, have a clear mindset for what you want to achieve by the end of your live stream. Often, people begin a live stream blindly, which will mean your Instagram video will likely achieve very little.

Quality is critical when it comes to Instagram. Up to 67 percent of Instagram viewers perceive quality as the first thing when considering which videos to watch. The kind of equipment and sound system matters a lot. Ensure that the sound and clarity of your video is excellent.

Instagram live streaming boosts your confidence. If you are the kind of marketer who has low self-esteem, Instagram live streaming will help change that for the better. By continually showing your live videos to the world, those positive comments will help to turn around any negative beliefs in yourself.

Twitch Live is not among the most popular platforms in the world. When it comes to this platform, influencers matter a lot. Since Twitch is all about gaming, influencers are experienced gamers. They are viewed as celebrities on this platform. As a marketer, these are the kind of people you will depend on for selling your brand to the world.

Compared to other live streaming platforms, Twitch offers marketers up to five hours of live streaming. As if that is not enough, viewers are given a chance to share their views on their live chat platform. Compared to other platforms, Twitch is more interactive.

When you are looking to promote your brand using Twitch Live streaming, consider the age brackets of your audience. Twitch is perfect for a relatively young audience between the ages of 16 and 30 years.

Gender is another significant factor; only 25 percent of total Twitch users are female. Keeping all of this in mind, your target audience should be males between the ages of 16 and 30 years.

Just like other live streaming platforms, quality content is key when it comes to YouTube. To get maximum viewership, ensure that what you are putting out there is of the highest quality, both audibly and visually. Any YouTube viewer will tell you the one feature they look for when choosing which live stream video to watch is quality.

Listening to your audience during live streaming on YouTube is important. This platform provides a chat box. This kind of feedback helps to improve the quality of the live stream. Take, for example, a case where a viewer tells you to set your microphone or camera properly. These are things you can adjust instantly whenever you get such a comment.

Live streaming on social media is one of the best things that have happened in the 21st century for many businesses. Moreover, many of them have seen a boost in awareness over time that has led to profits for their brand. Because of this, remember to work hard to keep your followers.

Social media marketing and live streaming is one of the greatest inventions of this decade. However, it could be improved by giving viewers the opportunity to automatically know the identity and the location from which one is live streaming to avoid confusion. This would also help to build trust between the buyer and the seller.

About Your FREE Sneak Peek

I hope you've enjoyed *Social Media Marketing Live,* but don't go away just yet!

If you stick around a bit longer, I'd like give you a quick sneak peek into another book from the ***Social Media Marketing Masterclass*** series.

The book is titled **Social Media Marketing Productivity Hacks:** *Beat Procrastination And Sell More By Using Time Management Strategies And Tools To Help Your Business Grow on Instagram, YouTube, Facebook And More in 2020*

Enjoy!

--

Social Media Marketing Productivity Hacks

Beat Procrastination And Sell More By Using Time Management Strategies And Tools To Help Your Business Grow on Instagram, YouTube, Facebook And More in 2020

By Rory Ames-Hyatt

·Introduction

Look around you.

There has been a change in the way we communicate. At one point, you could watch advertisements on television. The radio showed you quick snippets of promotions. Magazines showed models and products to you as you browsed their pages.

Not today.

You could be practically anywhere in the world. You could be flying at 31,000 feet. You could be viewing a mobile device in a movie theatre, much to everyone's chagrin. Or perhaps, you are on a boat out at sea.

In all of these locations, you can be bombarded with marketing promotions.

Today, you are more connected than ever. Through social media, you are never too far away from the next marketing campaign. In fact, one could say you are quite literally face-to-face with an advertisement.

However, with the advent of newer technologies for social media marketing, we need new tools. We need tools to help us manage our marketing efforts. We need tools for time management and effective teamwork. But we do not need these tools for large scale organizations. We need to provide these tools for small-scale businesses, entrepreneurs, and freelancers.

That is what you will find in this book.

You will find a lot of convenient platforms for creating ideas, for communicating with your team, for storage and time management; you will find them all here.

So as they say, without further ado, let us dive in.

1 Growth of Social Media

Social media marketing was born with the need to reach a growing number of people. Brands wanted to reach out to more people in new ways. Unlike television, newspapers, and other advertising mediums, you can personalize your messages on social media. With that being said, if you could reach the right target audience, you had a better chance to make a sale. And not just for the revenues. Brands started using social networking to address concerns, communicate with the audience, and build brand value and loyalty.

It was a virtually untapped market. But thanks to the growing number of users, businesses could no longer ignore the huge potential of social media marketing.

It can arguably be said that social media marketing, or advertising, started with Facebook launching 'Pages' in 2007. Brands, for the first time, were able to have a presence on the network. They could build their audience and convert them into customers. A new term was born—'cost per fan.' This received a further boost when Facebook allowed paid advertising. This form of advertising was tweaked over time to make the system even better.

Now, there is a demographic matching, marketplace, and a lot more features to make Facebook advertising very efficient. Twitter, too, launched the 'Promoted Tweet' in 2010. Instagram, Snapchat, Pinterest, and LinkedIn all have their advertising products now that businesses can use for promotions.

Today, you will find almost every business on social media—from large multinational conglomerates to the neighborhood grocery store. Successful businesses are using social media marketing for lead generation, research, branding, customer retention, and e-commerce.

New businesses and brands are launched on Facebook and on the other networks, revealing future plans and making announcements. Advertising, video, live streaming, demographic matching, and technology upgrades are some forms of technology available for businesses. These features help businesses find new and improved ways to reach out and market their brands.

Many businesses today adopt social media marketing to grant them a wider audience, better promotional capabilities, and the power of incredible reach. Gone are the days of spending enormous sums of money setting up billboards and hoping that your target audience will see them. Moreover, traditional forms of marketing do have the capacity to provide businesses with detailed insights. Everything seems rather arbitrary. How many people actually saw the billboard and reacted to it? Could businesses have paid the same amount and reached people through better means? Through social media, the time required to market services and products has been significantly reduced.

Customer service has improved. 83 percent of customers posting complaints on a website, like Twitter, receive a quick reply. With this, the overall customer satisfaction is also improved. Businesses are thus able to retain customers better.

80 percent of the US population is on social media. It's much the same everywhere in the Western and the developing or the developed world. 53 percent of people on social media are following a brand, but the popularity of social media and the impact on marketing is expected to be even greater in the next few years. With the growth of mobile technology, one can expect the reach of social advertising to increase tremendously. There was a time when owning a mobile gadget means shelling out big bucks to get cool features. However, these days you have manufacturers creating phones with incredible features at a portion of the cost of big-branded phones.

So, what is going to be the future of social media marketing? What are the emerging technologies, user habits, trends, and new features? How are businesses going to adapt to the changing world to boost their social media presence and marketing activities?

1Uses of Social Media

Getting Access to New Customers

There are billions of people around the world using some type of social platform or even multiple platforms. It has become a way for people to share and communicate with their friends on just about anything. There are swarms of new customers waiting on your business. They would talk about it, especially if they had a good experience with your products and services.

Customers or potential customers will also speak negatively about your business if they have had a bad experience. As a local business owner, you must have a plan in place for complaints. Many of the larger businesses like to engage and take care of customer issues on places like Twitter because of the convenience and ease of the platform.

As of September 2013, 72 percent of online adults were using social networking sites, according to the Pew Research Center. This is happening over just about every demographic regardless of circumstances. In addition, social media campaigns are more effective in generating quality leads. This information spells out the opportunity for local businesses.

Building and Engaging with Potential Customers

I can't express enough about the importance of building your audience first. Consumers won't buy much, if any at all, when they do not get your attention. There are many ways of doing this, such as sharing great content about your products or by asking questions.

"Great content" may throw some of you off a bit, but it's simple and here's an example. Let's say you have a bakery business in your town or city and you have an Instagram page. You already have one thousand plus followers for the page. That means a fair number of people will see your posts organically. You could use this to communicate more about your delightful baked goodies. You could also discuss the history of your products and how it came about, as an example. When users comment on your posts, be sure to respond and answer their questions if needed. Your customers or potential customers love to be engaged with and valued. In this way, you can use the platform to build trust with your customers.

Show Up in the Search Results

When you set up social profiles, some may show in the search results. The search results occur on search engines like Google, Bing, and Yahoo. This is important because you gain more awareness and direction people toward your products and services. Notice the URL bar (the box that shows "http://www.......com"), and look at the name of the user, which is typically found after the "....com/social-username." After you add your business name, chances are that your profile may appear in the search results when you begin social media marketing. This is a great way of getting organic traffic to your social media profile with a little ingenuity on your part.

You Can Access the Power of Mobile

Some business owners can easily be confused when they try to understand what mobile technology can really do for them. This is because they are told and pitched heavily on mobile apps.

Local businesses are searched for heavily on social media sites, such as Facebook, Twitter, Pinterest, and even Instagram, with mobile devices. The thing to remember is that your social media profiles within these platforms. Your profiles must be set up properly to enable geo or location features within those mobile platforms.

A local business can also benefit from many other features from a mobile platform. You can easily integrate with social media, including email marketing and text messaging. You can use QR codes, mobile-optimized social campaigns (contests, surveys & games), and mobile coupons. The true benefit of mobile is that all of these benefits can be tracked for performance. This way, you can see all the available data and make conscious decisions overall.

The uses can seem endless when mobile is implemented properly with social media. Mobile cannot be ignored any longer, so position your local business now and don't wait to benefit from it. You can be the exception amongst your competitors in your local area. Learning how valuable mobile is supplies a great addition to your entire social media marketing strategy.

•Chapter 1: Why Productivity Is Key to Maximizing the ROI of Your Social Media Marketing Efforts

Many companies are doing very well with social media marketing these days. The perception is that only the big brands can succeed in this new wave of marketing, but that is a common misconception.

Any small business with a simple game plan can succeed in social media marketing. This is because it's much easier to manage expectations in your local market. Social media allows you to scale your business's marketing efforts. The competition in your local area is much, much lower. In fact, it doesn't matter if you are a local bakery in a city with 100 other bakeries, your chances of being visible with social media marketing are high in your own "backyard." Here's why: a large number of local businesses using social media aren't doing it right.

Your customers are using social media and are likely also using many other social platforms. Your business has potential customers looking for it within these different platforms, and you can reach them at minimal cost.

In fact, you could save a lot of money using social media marketing.

There are a few reasons for this.

1). Internet Access Is Spreading Rapidly

Wherever you decide to locate your business in the world, you can "connect" with your customers. Internet access is becoming simpler by the second and making social media accessible. That might not be a revelation, but as a small business owner, you have to recognize and adapt to it.

More and more people - even in remote areas - are gaining internet access. Fiber optics and satellite internet services are technologies making this possible. This is happening all over the world with high frequency. With internet access, your customers are a click away from you. They can look for your products and services anywhere, and at any time.

What's more, you can reach out to them, as well. You can perform effective customer service through your social platforms. You can even make sales happen! Most consumers are comfortable with businesses in their own communities, which is why reaching out to them is not that difficult. It only requires a strong social presence.

2). The Mobile Wave Is Here to Stay

Mobile is getting bigger by the minute. Think of all the smartphones available in the market. You have high-end models with a rather high price tag, and then you have cheaper alternatives packed with a lot of features.

With this, you have people across the globe connected via a mobile device. According to Statista, the world's mobile population reached 3.7 billion users in a January 2018 data collection. That's almost half the world's population. In other words, every other person on the planet has a mobile device.

Mobile marketing can be beneficial for your business and has the power to take it to another level. Your customers have mobile devices and are using them all the time. One might even say that it consumes their identity to a degree.

We need and cherish our mobile devices. We depend on them for just about everything because of convenient services and apps. Many people spend countless hours on their mobile devices using social media sites.

Local business owners would never imagine the importance of mobile marketing as a way to catapult their business. "Social is Mobile and Mobile is Local," is the motto here. You can't have one without the other if you want to compete locally.

Social media sites, such as Facebook, Twitter, Instagram, Periscope, Snapchat, WhatsApp, and even Pinterest, have location-based features. With these features, users can find you even as they pass by your place of business.

You practically have a two-pronged attack opportunity. One, you can use marketing to reach out to users. Secondly, you can make yourself visible to nearby people.

That is what social media gives you: the power to be aware.

3). Modern-Day Distribution Is Incredible

Thirty years ago, distribution with just about any medium was way too expensive. Publishing a book, distributing any news source, etc. were all expensive endeavors. It was nearly impossible to do these things on a budget. Fast forward to current times, and you will see that it's unbelievably accessible.

I like to categorize distribution into four categories: easy, free, cheap, and targeted.

Easy

These days, all you need is internet access and a PC or mobile device. With just a social platform and an identity, you are ready to start selling or promoting. There are many social media sites to access nowadays. They are very easy to use, as well.

Free

Distributing content is free when you use social media to share with an audience. Thus, this accessibility is far more effective.

There is one fact that many people share in this world; free is good. Most people will opt to use a free tool they can sign up for by providing simple information. With social media, such a process is available.

Cheap

This is the one where I always get a reaction of, "Huh?" Yes... cheap! Distribution of content can be cheap when using for marketing purposes. You can see this in PPC or pay-per-click advertising on social media sites. In a pay-per-click advertising model, you only pay when you receive clicks on your ad. Two of the most effective social media sites for that are Facebook and YouTube. And on these platforms, it is not very expensive to use PPS advertising.

Targeted

The most exciting part of distributing content in current times is the ability to target. As a business owner, only you know who your customers are. After using the analytics from a few of your social media sites, you know how to reach your customers. In some cases, you will be able to pinpoint exactly where to find these customers, as well.

Now, you might think that with all this connectivity, your task is now easy. You just need to bombard people will your promotions and voila! Instant awareness. You can almost imagine the sound of the cash register!

But the reality is different. You see, it is one thing to reach out to people, yet it is quite another to make that reach profitable. You could have thousands of people see your social media ads, but what is the point if only 30 people show up at your business location?

This is where productivity comes in.

Time for a crash course.

In business, productivity is simply the difference between input and output. Basically, how much do you put into your efforts to generate a desired result? It is an indication of the efficiency in a process.

Now, let's try seeing how productivity helps you, both in your business and in social media marketing:

Your process will be efficient.

Worrying about why it takes time to get things done? Now you know. Having a productive mindset lets you accomplish more, but the difference is that you will be generating quality output.

You can accomplish more.

Time is money. In business, that is not a philosophical quote, it is a principle. So with having the right influx of productivity, you can complete more tasks within the time you have.

Accomplishing more means more money.

Once again, time is money. When more tasks get done, you are on the track to completing more sales orders. And more sales bring in more dollars in the bank.

Group morale.

It is all about teamwork these days. However, if you are the only one putting in effort, what is the point of teamwork? Productivity increases group morale and that, in return, improves output.

Customer expectations.

At the end of the day, you need to keep customers satisfied. You need them to return to you. That happens if you have high-quality products. With increased productivity, you keep your products or services in the best quality. This has a wonderful effect on customer expectations; they begin to expect the best from you.

You save money.

You need to pay your employees. That becomes part of your expenses. However, through productivity, you get more output for the same time. Your employees are paid the same, but they give out more. That saves money. Think of it this way, imagine your employees are generating less for the same salary. Technically, your cost of production has increased.

You and your team can have a personal life.

Your team needs to stay motivated. So do you. A lack of personal life will only serve to demotivate you and everyone else. Through productive work, you get tasks done on time. This leaves time for extracurricular activities and allow you to tend to your personal affairs.

Sense of accomplishment.

If there is a lack of progress, then everyone feels the pressure of disappointment. Every business should show progress, however big or small it is. By completing things on time, you feel a sense of accomplishment. This motivates your team to work harder.

You meet deadlines.

In the corporate world these days, every goal has a deadline. If your productivity is low, you cannot reach those deadlines. Every deadline missed is an opportunity lost. Every opportunity is a potential to make money.

Meeting demands.

At the end of the day, customer demands have to be met. When you know that the market has more demand for your product, why produce less? Realize that customer demands do not exist for long. They eventually wane and dissipate. You only get one opportunity to make the most out of it.

Get Your Copy Of: **Social Media Marketing Productivity Hacks**

If you've enjoyed this free sneak peak into *Social Media Marketing Productivity Hacks*, then you can find the full book at all good book stores!

References

Laubscher, H. (2018). Twitch: The Unlikely But Important Amazon Business – AW360. Retrieved from https://360.advertisingweek.com/twitch-unlikely-important-amazon-business/

Nawrocki, S. (2018). Avoid These 13 Live Streaming Video Mistakes. Retrieved from https://video.ibm.com/blog/streaming-video-tips/avoid-these-13-live-streaming-video-mistakes/

Push Notifications Explained | Urban Airship. (2019). Retrieved from https://www.urbanairship.com/push-notifications-explained

Traditional Media vs. Social Media Advertising - Cost Comparison. (2018). Retrieved from https://www.lyfemarketing.com/traditional-media-versus-social-media/

Twitch.tv - Partners. (2019). Retrieved from https://www.twitch.tv/p/partners/

What Is SEO / Search Engine Optimization? - Search Engine Land. (2019). Retrieved from https://searchengineland.com/guide/what-is-seo

- -